FROM AUDEN TO YEATS
Critical Analysis Of 30 Selected Poems

GEETANJALI MUKHERJEE

Also by the Author

Seamus Heaney: Select Poems, Rama Bros. India.
Will The Real Albert Speer Please Stand Up? The Many Faces of Hitler's Architect.
Illusions: A Collection of Poetry.
Creating Consensus: The Journey Towards Banning Cluster Munitions
Anyone Can Get An A+: How To Beat Procrastination, Reduce Stress and Improve Your Grades
Anyone Can Get An A+ Companion Workbook: How To Beat Procrastination, Reduce Stress and Improve Your Grades

From Auden to Yeats: Critical Analysis of 30 Selected Poems
By Geetanjali Mukherjee

Copyright © 2010 Geetanjali Mukherjee

Current Print Edition published with Createspace, March 2017.

First Edition, 2010 [From Auden to Yeats: Critical Analysis of Selected British Poetry]

Cover Image: Salvatore Vuono / FreeDigitalPhotos.net
Book and Cover Design: Geetanjali Mukherjee

All rights reserved. No part of this publication may be reproduced, distributed, or transmitted in any form or by any means, including photocopying, recording, or other electronic or mechanical methods, without the prior written permission of the publisher.

To my parents Ratna and Ashish Mukherjee, who taught me a love of literature and a belief in the value of education, for oneself and others.

TABLE OF CONTENTS

INTRODUCTION 1
WYSTAN HUGH AUDEN 3
    Lullaby 5
    Dear, Though The Night Is Gone 7
    Musee Des Beaux Arts 9
    Epitaph On A Tyrant 11
    Refugee Blues 13
    The Unknown Citizen 15
    Miss Gee 17
TED HUGHES 22
    Crow Tyrannosaurus 25
    Full Moon And Little Frieda 27
    The Thought-Fox 28
    The Stag 31
    Wind 33
JOHN KEATS 36
    On First Looking Into Chapman's Homer 39
    Last Sonnet 40
    La Belle Dame Sans Merci 42
    To Autumn 44
PHILIP LARKIN 47
    Poetry Of Departures 50

The Building 53
Wild Oats 56
Church Going 58
Reasons For Attendance... 62
The Whitsun Weddings 63
Dockery and Son 66
W. B. YEATS.. 70
He Wishes For The Cloths Of Heaven 73
Song Of Wandering Aengus 74
Adam's Curse... 76
Wild Swans At Coole... 79
Broken Dreams 81
The Second Coming 83
A Prayer For My Daughter 86
STUDY GUIDE... 90
ACKNOWLEDGEMENTS 109
ABOUT THE AUTHOR 110

INTRODUCTION

I WAS INTRODUCED TO the writings of these five eminent poets as a seventeen-year old in high school, and approached their work with a mixture of awe and apprehension. While I found their poetry beautiful, I was daunted by the prospect of interpreting their poetry and writing papers on them. The words loomed large on the page and threatened to overwhelm, and I all but dropped the class.

Fortunately, I persevered, and came to love and appreciate the works of these and other talented poets. I also overcame my apprehension of writing papers on these poems. Like me, perhaps many of you also feel apprehensive about interpreting difficult poems, dissecting them and finding meaning in them. I wrote this book for you. I wrote it keeping in mind students who need a head start in finding their feet, who need a push in the right direction. This book is for the student who can read the analyses given here, and use it as a base for their own interpretations, their own analysis. This book is not intended as a cheat sheet, so that you can simply copy the essays given here in lieu of actually doing the work yourself. I intend these essays as a starting point, as a launching pad for your own thoughts and ideas.

In the beginning of each section, I have included a short biography of each poet. I have included only the basic details of their lives, and any snippets that may help to shed light on their work. This is only the tip of the iceberg, using the internet it is possible to find out a great deal more. While writing their biographies I was fascinated by the lives of Keats, Auden, Hughes and the others, inspired by their commitment to keep writing amidst adversity, encouraged by their ability to break through criticism and failure to reach success. I hope through this book to introduce you to some of the twentieth centuries' best poets, as well as show you what is possible if only we can tap into that which is great in each of us. I wish you luck in all you do, and may the literary greats watch over you.

WYSTAN HUGH AUDEN

BIOGRAPHY OF W.H. AUDEN

WYSTAN HUGH AUDEN WAS born on 21 February 1907 in York, England. He grew up in Birmingham, the third of three children, three boys. His father was a physician, and his mother was trained as a nurse. Whilst Auden was interested in science as a boy, he studied English literature at Christ Church, Oxford. In Oxford, he became part of a group of left-wing intellectuals including Cecil Day Lewis and Christopher Isherwood, who formed what was known as "the Auden generation".

Auden published his first book of poems at the age of twenty-one, a slim volume printed by a friend. This was an immediate success. A year later Faber and Faber published the volume *Poems*, and then *The Orators*, in 1932. Auden's writing was starkly different, and provided a political voice that stood out against the turbulent times. In 1935, Auden married Erika Mann, to help her escape from Nazi Germany. In the following years, Auden travelled with friends, writing more volumes, till he eventually ended up in the United States. Auden's popularity grew in the States, and in 1946, he became a US citizen.

In America, he had a relationship for 20 years with a composer Chester Kallman, for whom he wrote opera librettos. The years after he moved to America became Auden's most productive period. The first book of poems he published in America was *Another Time*, in 1941, containing some of his most beautiful poems. He began to move away from religious and political themes. In 1948, he published *The Age of Anxiety*, for which he was awarded the Pulitzer Prize. In 1953, he received the prestigious Bollingen Award, regarded by then as one of the most notable poets of his generation. Auden died in Vienna, Austria, in 1973.

W.H. Auden was not only a poet; he was also a librettist, playwright, essayist and scholar. Auden moved away from the Romantic style of poetry as typified by Keats or Shelley and was influenced by literary Modernism, and writers like T.S. Eliot. He relied heavily on imagery in his poetry, and wrote many poems that focused on intense feelings and emotions. His poems were often cryptic and difficult to understand, but the beauty of his writing gripped his readers nonetheless. He explored the arenas of religion, science and philosophy in his work, lending his poems a realistic quality. Not only was Auden one of the greatest poets of the 20th century, he changed the landscape of poetry forever.

CRITICAL ANALYSIS OF SELECTED POEMS

Lullaby

Auden believed that love is a powerful, creative force; it must be disciplined and controlled, otherwise it becomes a powerful force for destruction. It becomes self-love, an inhibiting force. Yet the ideal love is that in which the self does not love its importance, by being merged into a larger unit, the new relationship includes and transcends the old one. "Lullaby" is a poem essentially about the metaphysical and spiritual aspect of love.

The tone of the poem is tender and lyrical, reinforcing the subject, which is serious. It is in the form of a dramatic monologue, addressed by the speaker to his love. The poem is weighty with thought, moving away from convention, and imbibing the simplicity of a true lyric. The rhymes are delicately hinted, creating a harmony between musical lines and extended statements, which reinforces the poem's gravity.

The opening is abrupt and colloquial, spoken by a lover to his sleeping love. There is a realistic approach to the lover's words, he has no illusions about himself, knows that he is "faithless". He talks of love as "ephemeral"; it will "burn away" with time. He does not glorify his beloved as a goddess and put her on a pedestal, he recognises that she is merely "mortal, guilty", and accepts her the way she is, "entirely beautiful". He knows that disease, old age and death are the only permanent and universal facts. Their love too is subject to death and decay. In the same way he accepts his lover, man should accept life with all its imperfections.

During the ecstasy of sexual fulfilment, in their "ordinary swoon", the lovers seem to break the bounds of "soul and body", and become one, fused with each other. Their "casual ecstasy" is thus transformed into a spiritual union, a source of mystical bliss such as the hermit experiences in moments of mystical union with God. The supernatural inspiration sent out by Venus transforms them, and their ecstasy and the "abstract insight" of the hermit have no essential difference. Their sexual love is thus transformed into "universal love and hope".

Auden here displays the fact that he has no illusions about the permanence of sexual love. Sexual love is merely physical and it dies as soon as the enjoyment is over, "on the stroke of midnight pass". It is now fashionable to condemn sexual love because it is short-lived by "pedantic boring" men. The lovers have to pay "every farthing of the cost", the price for sexual fulfilment is the suffering and indifference that comes with it. "Not a kiss nor look be lost" now, as from this night the lovers will grow indifferent to each other.

With the morning comes disillusionment, and all their "visions" of love and beauty come to an end. These concluding lines constitute the prayer of the lover for the future happiness of the beloved. The lover says, the fountains of love will dry up in their hearts, "noons of dryness"; and they will become spiritually wretched and miserable. Auden suggests only one cure for this dryness. Reassured by "eye and knocking heart" that they still have a beautiful world to live in, they should "find [the] mortal world enough", accept it as a great blessing and thank "the involuntary powers" for it. Then by providence, fountains of love will pour out of their hearts for God who has blessed them in this way. God will inspire them with love for their fellow creatures, "human love"; allow "nights of insult" to pass them, and this alone can protect them from the worries of the world. This poem is a message of universal love - accept the world as it is and as a great blessing.

Dear, Though The Night Is Gone

This poem illustrates Auden's concept of the difference between selfish love and agape, or universal love. The poem is a dramatic monologue, the recounting of their relationship ending, presumably by the man. In this relationship, he represents universal, unselfish love. The tone of the poem is soft and gentle, even though his lover has left him, he does not speak harshly. She, his lover, on the other hand, is representative of the selfish kind of love. It is a bitter-sweet love poem, ending in an unexpected twist, but with typical Auden subtlety.

The poem is written in three octets, and the rhyme scheme is *ABCDDCAB*, an unusual one. The tone of the poem is conversational and easy, there is no harshness or bitterness in the voice of the speaker, only a nostalgic note. The poem ends with a characteristic understatement by Auden.

The speaker is recounting the night of passion after waking up, and though the night is gone, "its dream still haunts to-day". The night is symbolic of mystery, passion and romance, all that has gone out of the relationship they shared, which has now ended. An Auden simile, "lofty as a railway terminus", describes the setting, where many beds were, and they were "crowded in that gloom", yet isolated because of their love for each other.

They spent a private moment together, disturbing on one, "[their] whispers woke no clocks". His was an unquestioning, unconditional love, "glad at everything [she] did". They were "indifferent" to those who watched them with bitterness, hostility or envy, "inert and vaguely sad", as the love had gone out of their relationships. Those people were now unhappy, even though they were together. He in fact is insecure, and feels that society is frowning on their relationship, but her kisses quell his fears.

The speaker asks her why she left him, he asks whether there was something lacking in him, that she made him the victim of a "hidden worm of guilt". Without feeling ashamed, "unabashed", she "confessed another love", and left the relationship. She did what he never would have wished, and hurt him terribly. He then, "submissive", "felt unwanted", and left, the room and the relationship.

Auden in this poem contrasts the two kinds of love, selfish and unconditional. Even though the man's love was unconditional, the woman's love was selfish and did not last. Thus, their relationship broke off. The dream that started out beautifully ended up as a painful memory to the speaker. Although he played down the pain, it hurt him deeply.

Musee Des Beaux Arts

The title of the poem refers to the Museum of Fine Arts in Brussels, which Auden visited in the winter of 1938. He was attracted by the paintings of Brueghel, which inspired Auden to write this poem. The poem juxtaposes ordinary and extraordinary events; however, the extraordinary events seem to lose their importance in his descriptions. The theme of the poem is the indifference of humanity to the fact of individual suffering. The tone of the poem is conversational and informal, almost as if Auden were talking to a friend or thinking aloud. The poem is a collection of unlike sounds, and it suggests a religious acceptance of suffering, rather than criticism. It is a satire on the callous attitude to the suffering of others in the modern age.

Auden says that "the Old Masters" rightly understood the nature of human suffering, and depicted it faithfully. Their paintings reveal that they understood that while individuals suffer, life goes on for the rest as usual, eating, walking or going along their daily tasks. The old religious-minded people wait with devotion and enthusiasm for "the miraculous birth", and there are always children to whom it does not matter, who "did not specially want it to happen". They are indifferent and go back to their games and activities.

"They" could be referring to Brueghel or the great painters in general. Auden points out that in Brueghel's painting "The Massacre of Innocents", as the crucifixion of Christ was taking place, "the dogs go on with their doggy life", and the horse of the torturer "scratches its innocent behind on a tree". He shows how these creatures are completely unconcerned with Jesus' suffering.

In the painting "Icarus", the artist depicts the fall of the boy into the ocean, as a farmer and ship watch in amazement. The ploughman may have heard the splash, but he did not even look up from his work, as "it was not an important failure" to him. The "expensive delicate ship" that saw the boy's fall, "had somewhere to get to" and sailed on, unconcerned. None of them made any attempt to rescue him, and went on with their routine activities.

Both instances were path-breaking events – the crucifixion of Christ and the failure of the first attempt to fly – and both went blissfully unheeded, only later did people realise the importance of these events. Auden depicts here how human suffering goes unnoticed by the indifferent populace. There is a sort of continuity depicted through the two poems, and the reader becomes more aware of his "human position". Despite the instances of indifference and callousness showed in the two events, the poem is not critical of human nature; it is more accepting of human suffering and the reaction to it.

Epitaph On A Tyrant

Auden studied at Oxford University, where he began to establish his reputation as a leading poet. During the thirties, he described it as "a time of crisis and dismay". In Britain, millions were unemployed, and Hitler was rising to power in Germany. This is probably when he wrote the poem, 'Epitaph on a Tyrant', expressing some of the social and political problems he experienced as a young man. The problems of the times and his own political beliefs influenced his poetry to a large extent.

Hitler's cruel treatment of the Jews influenced the thinking of many poets of the time, Auden even more so. This sestet has been written as a poem that Auden would have engraved in Hitler's tombstone. Its rhyme scheme *ABBCAC* is simple enough. At a first reading, the real meaning of the poem does not emerge till the last line, but subtle undertones reveal much more than is at first obvious.

Hitler's assertion that the Aryans are the most perfect race, and that the world should be rid of Jews, is played upon by Auden, as "perfection, of a kind, was what he was after" suggests. "Of a kind" suggests that Hitler's idea of perfection was warped and undesirable. His "poetry", or oratorical skills, were "easy to understand", as they appealed to the masses. As a result, Hitler amassed a huge fan following in Germany, coupled with his vibrant personality and power to charm audiences with his words. He understood "human folly" or human nature completely, and knew how to phrase something to make the greatest impact. He was "greatly interested in armies and fleets", more a general of war than of peace. His power lay in the sycophancy of "respectable senators", who were completely in his power.

Auden writes, that when Hitler cried, "little children died in the streets". This surprise twist reveals the true meaning of the poem, and points directly to the fact that Hitler was terribly cruel. His terrible killing of the Jews and the holocaust are almost predicted here, although Hitler's actions would be plain to the world many years later.

Although the poem appears to be straightforward, there are hidden meanings in the lines. Hitler is not directly labelled as cruel till the last line, but on a closer reading it is apparent as an undercurrent throughout the poem. This short poem aptly brings out Hitler's characteristics, and does ample credit to Auden's literary style.

Refugee Blues

This poem was published in 1939, before the Holocaust had begun. It is surprisingly reflective of a premonition as well as his sensitivity to the plight of the Jews. It is a blues poem, and one of lament, cataloguing the plight of the refugees and the selfishness of citizens safe in their "mansions".

Auden was experimenting with the blues style, which expresses a social or personal cause of grief. The third line of every verse has the same structure, to bring out the human sentiment, while the first two lines contrasts with the situation, etching out the sorry plight. The poet uses repetition successfully in the poem for emphasis.

The poetic voice or speaker laments the fact that a city of ten million people cannot find any shelter for them, "no place for us". The speaker is one-half of a Jewish couple that had immigrated to the US. They talk next of their native country Germany, a place they found "fair", however they were not allowed to return there.

The churchyard in the village houses a beautiful old yew, which "blossoms anew" every spring. Even though it is a place of burial and death, life springs there again.

However, they cannot renew their citizenship. The consul at the embassy "banged the table" and rudely informed them that they were "officially dead", although they were still alive.

Wherever the couple went they were politely or hostilely told to leave, "come back next year"; "if we let them in, they will steal our daily bread". Auden is mocking the hymn of the Lord which says, "give us today our daily bread". These statements today remind us of arguments against immigration and globalisation in many countries, and the hostile attitude that many people hold against immigrants, many of them fleeing political unrest and persecution like the couple in the poem. When Hitler said, with "thunder rumbling in the sky", that "they must die", he had the German Jews in his mind. The poem goes on to say that whilst even dogs and cats were looked after in the United States, the Jews are not. The fish in the harbour swam "as if they were free", and they were only a few feet away from the imprisoned couple, imprisoned by their circumstances. The poet is also commenting on how nature is carefree, and the birds "sang at their ease". The natural world has no hierarchy like the humans, and they are given their own space. The poem contrasts the harmony and freedom in nature with the manmade bonds that restrict the couple.

The speaker dreamed that he saw a building "with a thousand floors"; however, "not one of them was ours". The dream signified freedom of choice, choice to decide where to live, choice to live on their own terms, choices that the couple have been denied. Instead, they are discarded and removed from all proofs of existence. The image contrasts the "ten thousand soldiers" and "the falling snow", juxtaposing the purity of the snow and the evil of the soldiers. The soldiers were looking for the refugees. Both images are seen as if at a distance, and the snow also implies a covering for the dead.

In this poem, the pathos of the Jews is clearly revealed. It is an important and disturbing topic that has even more relevance today. Auden's light-hearted and yet emotive treatment of the subject touches the reader's heart.

The Unknown Citizen

Auden was against the idea of fascism, the idea of burying the individual for the sake of the collective consciousness. In this poem, he depicts the degree of dehumanization taking place, an ironical picture of a model citizen in a modern urbanized society. This person has nothing extraordinary, nothing unique other than facts and figures to remember him by, and no one really knew anything about him. The question posed by the poet in the end is the crux of the poem.

'The Unknown Citizen', like many of Auden's other poems, is written in a conversational style, belying the serious nature of the theme. The epigraph is the reproduction of his epitaph, a series of numbers and letters, "erected by the state". He had no family to speak of, no one to care enough even to inscribe his name onto his epitaph.

The poet goes on to say that the Bureau of Statistics found no criminal records in his name, "no official complaint". From all his reports, it is evident that he was a modern-day saint, as he "served the greater community". Till the outbreak of the war, he worked all his life in an absurd company called Fudge Motors Inc. The absurd name highlights the absurdity of the situation. He was neither a "scab" nor a rebel, and was always socially correct, but never took a stand. He never incurred any debts, was liked by his office mates and "liked a drink". He was the model social being, an epitome of the model citizen, and led a completely ordinary life.

The citizen bought a paper each day, had the "normal" reactions, was fully insured, and had only been ill once. All government departments declare that his standard of living was correct, neither above nor below his means. He had all the required attributes "necessary to the Modern Man". He had the right political opinions, married and had five children, "the right number". He educated them in the right way and never "interfered". He always did the right thing at the right time. However, the important question is "was he free? Was he happy?" The question is "absurd", as we need not worry, if anything was wrong, the department would have the statistics. The poet is being ironic here.

The poem attacks the concept of a human being not being more than a product of the economic, commercial and ideological groups he belongs to. Society forces him to conform to standard patterns of life and thought, forces uniformity on the individual. Auden protests against this dehumanization of society, where a man is reduced to a compilation of statistics, and people are indifferent to a person's real lives and problems. The poem is written in a flat, matter-of-fact style, highlighting the fact that nothing is or should be flat and matter-of-fact, least of all in human relations.

Miss Gee

In the poem "Miss Gee", written in 1937, Auden has displayed his interest in the individual human being, and individual suffering. He was also significantly influenced by Freud and his theory of Eros, the sex-instinct. This erotic instinct, healthy if controlled, becomes self-destructive if suppressed. Thus, according to Auden, in Miss Gee, the virgin who is denied sexual gratification, the unfulfilled instinct produces her own cancer.

"Miss Gee" was written in the traditional ballad form. It is in quatrains with alternate rhymes, and the language is simple and easy to understand. The light-hearted structure of the ballad belies the underlying pathos of her life. It is a comic treatment of a serious subject, and the comedy enhances the tragedy of the situation. The poem is an honest presentation of human suffering and it recognises the element of cruelty in our social behaviour.

The reader is introduced to Miss Gee of 83, Clevedon Terrace, as a lonely, repressed spinster. "Number 83" suggested that there were at least eighty-two other such houses, and portrays a box-like image, highlighting the insignificance of her existence. The poet seemed to make fun of her appearance, presenting a degrading point of view. She had a "slight squint" in her left eye, and her appearance was unattractive and diffident; "she had no bust at all". This is descriptive of the voice of society, the way they degrade her and laugh at her.

Miss Gee wore cheap, tough clothes made of serge, highlighting her poverty. Just like the enduring serge, she endures on, as a borderline survivor, putting on a tough exterior. Her clothes are symbolic of how she tries to blend in, and stands out even more. The colours of purple and green mentioned by the poet symbolise royalty and envy, respectively. The "harsh back-pedal brake" implies the harshness of her denial of sexual pleasures, and the extent of her repressions.

Miss Gee's only escape route was the Church. She knitted for the Church Bazaar of Saint Aloysius, which provided her with a private income, and was also charitable work. She often longed to belong, to have more meaning in her life. She was hungry for love, her repression is implied through a suggestion that she could not sleep at night. "Looking upset at the starlight", she questioned the powers that be – did anyone care about her? She lived in genteel poverty, "on one hundred pounds a year". Her repression came out in a dream about the only man she had ever come into contact with; she dreamt that "she was the Queen of France" and the Vicar asked her to dance. A storm blew about the palace, she was "biking through a field of corn", and a bull with the face of the Vicar was charging at her, with the force of her sexual repression. She could feel him behind her, and would have succumbed to his passion, if not for that "back-pedal brake". Her hunger for love and company was manifesting itself in the dream, and the image of the bull lends a comic touch with cruel undertones to her dream. Miss Gee longed for importance, and linked it with the only man she knew, yet repressed her feelings because of the conflict she felt between her desires and her conscience.

The ice-age imagery of the poem shows the spiritual decay of the age. This idea is carried by the fact that Miss Gee "buttoned [her clothes] up to her neck", signifying her outward show of modesty and propriety. She "turned her head away" from loving couples, just as love turned its head away from her. Her role in life was passive, that of an observer. She prayed to God to "make [her] a good girl, please"; trying to ignore the conflict in her mind, as she felt moved by violent sexual passion and needed God's guidance to save her from going astray.

Time was passing Miss Gee by, and it was unleashing "waves" of passion, that could either wreak her reputation or her health. Her outward modesty made it difficult for her to allow a male doctor to examine her, and she did not want to spend the money on herself, perhaps as she believed that she was not worth it. As the doctor discussed her condition with his wife over dinner, his air was detached and impersonal, as if discussing a hypothetical case rather than a real human being. Auden here uses a typical original simile to describe the effects of cancer, "like some hidden assassin / waiting to strike at you". In a vivid, violent image, the simile tells its own story. The doctor then went on to say that "childless women" and "men when they retire" get this disease, due to a need to vent their "creative fire". He was commenting on the unhappiness of people who do not have a mission, which negatively impacts their whole life, even their health. However, here the doctor's simple and deceptive comment shows the apathy of human society. The collective consciousness of people is not affected by the genuine pain of a fellow human being.

The poem goes on to narrate that Miss Gee was taken to a hospital, "a goner", and lay in the women's ward, where the doctor displayed the advanced degree of her sarcoma, as "the students began to laugh". The degree of dehumanization and disrespect for her was heightened in the hospital. The surgeon had reduced her to a cancerous growth, not a human being.

She was then "wheeled away", to the Department of Anatomy, where "a couple of Oxford Groupers carefully dissected her knee". This was the perfunctory way she was disposed with. There was no one to bother with her, as she had no money for a proper burial. She was treated as if she had committed some crime by donating her body for research. Not a single student cared who she was, where she had come from, she was simply a specimen to them.

In the poem, "Miss Gee", Auden has poignantly brought out the degree of dehumanisation society was brought to, and his light-hearted treatment of the subject simply underscored the point and further roused the reader's sympathy.

TED HUGHES

BIOGRAPHY OF TED HUGHES

TED HUGHES OR EDWARD JAMES HUGHES was a renowned English poet and children's writer. He was a British Poet Laureate from 1984 until his death in 1998. He was born in Mytholmroyd, Yorkshire, in 1930. Hughes attended Pembroke College in Cambridge, initially studying English literature, but later switching to anthropology. He met his future wife and American poet Sylvia Plath at Cambridge, eventually marrying her in 1956. Plath and Hughes moved to the United States in 1957, and lived there for two years, after which they moved back to England.

Hughes' marriage was far from happy, and following his affair with Assia Wevill, Plath and Hughes ended their marriage in 1962. They had two children, Frieda and Nicholas. A short time later, in 1963, Plath committed suicide, cutting short what could have been an even more remarkable career as a poet and writer. Following Plath's death, Wevill moved in with Hughes and his children, and even had a daughter with him. They never married, to her chagrin, and Hughes maintained affairs with other women. In 1969, Wevill killed her daughter Shura and committed suicide, in a manner remarkably similar to Plath's own death. The suicide of both women and the manner of their death has led to innumerable controversies and conspiracy theories, and it is impossible to ever know the real nature of Hughes' relationships with them. Hughes remarried in 1970, to Carol Orchard, a nurse, and they were together till Hughes' death in 1998. He died of heart failure, after suffering from colon cancer, at the age of 68.

Hughes has been regarded as one of the greatest poets of the twentieth century by critics and his contemporaries. Before he died, he received the prestigious Order of Merit from Queen Elizabeth II. In his early work, he wrote extensively about nature and both the beauty and violence inherent in nature. He used animals as metaphors for human beings, as seen in the poems 'Crow Tyrannosaurus', or 'The Thought-Fox'. He also wrote about the cruelty of human beings as inflicted on nature, as in 'The Stag'. Hughes also wrote several translations of European plays as well as poetry for children.

Of all the poets whose poems appear in this volume, Hughes has been attacked the most severely about his personal life, especially by fans of Plath's writing. He has been portrayed as an arrogant and uncaring man who led two women to suicide and deprived the world of a feminist and writer like Plath. Hughes had added to that image by destroying some of Plath's writings and maintaining an aloof and almost unfeeling silence regarding his life with Plath. However, it is difficult to really know what the truth about Plath's death and their relationship was. In a cruel twist of fate, in March 2009, Hughes' son with Plath, Nicholas Hughes, committed suicide after battling severe depression. Undoubtedly a talented man, Ted Hughes has been dogged by controversy, both in life and in death.

CRITICAL ANALYSIS OF SELECTED POEMS

Crow Tyrannosaurus

The crow is an animal featuring in many of Hughes' poems. He used animals as metaphors to bring out certain characteristics or defects of human beings, and he wrote more than one volume of poems with a crow as the protagonist or at least featuring in the poem. The crow symbolized the human being, and had primarily man's devilish nature embodied in it. In this poem, "Crow Tyrannosaurus", the crow's internal battle symbolized the battle of the human being who was battling within himself the thought of vegetarianism, and was losing the battle.

The larger part of the poem is in quatrains, where the poet discusses the advantages of vegetarianism and recounts the horrors of the dead creatures. However, when the crow lost its battle, the ordered structure of his debate, and the poem, disintegrated, breaking up into single lines and phrases. The imagery is stark and realistic, the reader can imagine the "blurt of all those voices".

The sounds "of mourning and lament" that the crow could hear were made by nature's creations, lamenting the "cortege". There were sounds of death and destruction everywhere. He could hear the "anguish" of the insects the swift had eaten, as its "pulsating" body flew past him. The body of the cat "withered", its throat a "gagging" tunnel, "of incoming death-struggles", as the dying things it had eaten were choking the cat. The dog was filtering all the death and destruction it had caused, all the animals "gulped for the flesh and bones". The cry of the dog was a "blout", a mixture of "all those voices". Even man was a "walking abbatoir", a slaughterer of all the innocent animals he had killed. His brain was burning the cries of their outcries.

The crow was debating within himself, whether he should "stop eating" other animals, and try to "become the light", or become enlightened. He symbolised the unfortunate human being, who was battling the urge to slaughter innocents for food and instead follow a more humane path. The crow immediately lost the battle however, as he saw a grub. Instantly his "trap sprung" and he stabbed the grub. Then he listened. "And he heard weeping". He stabbed, and listened, and heard the grub weeping. The spacing of the poem showed his hesitation, his feelings, as he disliked what he was doing, and then went ahead and did it anyway. Finally, he completely ignored his inner voice, and killed the grub. Then, he became blind, "the eye's roundness", and deaf, "the ear's deafness". The lineation is illustrating the fading away of consciousness, the distancing of the crow from his inner voice.

The poem further shows how killing is a part of life, but a horrific part nevertheless. Though in the animal kingdom killing is for survival, the poet also provides instances where killing is not necessity; it is sport, as in his poem "The Stag". Even here, he deplores the degeneration of the human being, who cannot hear pleas for help, or see misery. The crow as the symbol of the human itself speaks Hughes' disgust for the degeneration of human beings.

Full Moon And Little Frieda

Ted Hughes' had a daughter named Frieda, and he a son called Nicholas. According to his writing, Hughes had always been honest with his children, yet in his own way he tried to protect them. In the poem "Full Moon and Little Frieda", the child Frieda is amazed at beholding the full moon. Here, Hughes comments on how much a part of nature a child seems to be.

The tactile, sensuous imagery of the moonlit night further highlights the amazement and wonder of the little child. Rather than set out in precise stanzas, the poem is in the form of one flowing, disjointed stanza, mirroring the flowing moonlight, shedding light and warmth on everything. The lineation of the poem is important, especially in the last few lines, as it represents the stepping back of the moon, "gazing amazed" at his own masterpiece.

The "cool small evening" is serene and calm, and the child is listening, and observing. The spider in his web is tense, waiting for the dew to fall. The water in the pail shimmers, a mirror "to tempt a first star to a tremor".

The next image is a cosy one, the cows "are going home", ambling, their bells tinkling. The pathway seems like "a dark river of blood", reflecting the earth. The reflection of the moon on the boulders lends them a look of "balancing unspilled milk".

Suddenly the child cries out "Moon! Moon!" in wonder and amazement at the sight of a beautiful, round, luminous object, a circle of light shining up in the sky. The child's astonishment is mirrored in the moon, as he "has stepped back like an artist gazing amazed". He is amazed at the wonder of his own creation, "that points back at him amazed". On both sides there is equal astonishment and joy.

This poem is an effective counter to critics who brand Hughes as a rough, emotionless poet, as it brings out beauty and tenderness of a completely unique nature. The poem shows a father's pride and love in his daughter, as she discovers the beauty and wonder in the world around her.

The Thought-Fox

In "The Thought-Fox", Ted Hughes uses the metaphor of a fox to illustrate the art of writing a poem. This is his first animal poem, after which he wrote several volumes of poems to do with animals, often using animals as metaphors of qualities in humans.

The most striking quality of "The Thought-Fox" is its exquisite imagery. Hughes has an uncanny ability of transforming ordinary words or objects into a striking metaphor, for example, it is unusual to look at a fox's movements as the metaphor for the entrance of an idea in the mind. Hughes disregards strict rhyme and meter in the poem, and the rhythm stimulates the action. The swift, sudden trot, then the cautious tread, and the confident, even pace of the fox's movements echo the journey of an idea in the mind. The idea strikes suddenly, then cautiously grows, and then comfortably settles down, becoming a piece of written work.

The poem begins with a vivid image, the "mid-night moment's forest". It signifies the world of imagination and inspiration. The "clock's loneliness" echoes his own blankness, as he is unable to pen anything on "this blank page". He knows the idea is there somewhere, but it is eluding him, and not translating into words.

Something however is emerging slowly, "entering the loneliness", touching his mind. The ideas inside his mind are building up, and they are no longer far away; so he sees "no star". The tactile, sensuous images describe the entering of the idea, "delicately". The idea is not bold enough yet, like the cautious fox whose eyes "serve a movement", and slowly "sets neat prints in the snow", imprinting thoughts in the mind. It peeps "between trees", and is somewhat visible.

The idea is slowly reaching a height of fertility, and coming along fast. The "clearing" is a metaphor for the page where the poem is being written, and the "eye" is the insight of the poet. The "widening greenness" depicts the fertile mind of the poet, which is now "concentratedly" giving birth to an idea. Then, "with a sudden sharp stink of fox", the poem comes together, and "enters the dark hole of the head". The idea emerges entirely and takes shape. The "window is starless", and now there is no inspiration outside, it has been written on the paper, "the page is printed". The cyclical movement of the idea is symbolised by the clock, which was silent at first, then it ticked, and there was a lot of noise in the poet's mind. Now there is silence again, while "the clock ticks".

The appeal of the poem lies in its imagery and unusual juxtaposition of words and phrases, like "this midnight moment's forest", and "sudden sharp stink of fox". The average reader does not relate to the metaphor of the fox, and fails to completely comprehend the poem's meaning, but the tactile imagery makes an impact on him. Hughes' unusual and honest portrayal touches a chord within the reader, making this a well-loved poem.

The Stag

Hughes often uses animals and their characteristics to bring out certain qualities of the human race, as seen in the above poems. In the poem "Stag", he sets the scene of a stag hunt right outside a jail, a place where hardened, barbaric criminals are punished. His unusual juxtaposition highlights the barbarism of the stag hunt; at the same time it brings out the hypocrisy of human beings, as on one hand they lock up criminals, on the other they encourage this barbarism.

The poetic elements in the poem are understated rather than explicit. The imagery is stark, transporting the reader to the actual scene of the hunt. His winding, drawn-out descriptions of the humans are contrasted with his terse, confident, dignified comments on the stag's movements as he majestically runs "through his private forest".

The first image is of a rainy November afternoon, a cold and dreary day, in Exmoor, a jail in England. People are stopping to watch, causing a traffic jam. Farmers are hurriedly parking and "scrambling" to the top of the bank to look through the leafless forest. The majestic, dignified stag is running through its private territory. Hughes brings out effectively the indignity of being hunted for no rhyme or reason in its own territory.

The poet then describes the scene outside the forest. There are noisy, irritating sounds emanating from the ridiculous, self-absorbed people watching the hunt. The kids, "gossiping heads", "mothers and aunts and grandmothers", are all there to enjoy themselves, portraying an undignified, crass image. This is contrasted with the dignity with which the stag is running through his "favourite valley". Juxtaposition of these two different images heightens the cruelty of the act, done for "sport", and heightens the indignity of the human race, as opposed to the dignity of the stag.

The "blue horsemen" are advancing "down in the soggy meadow" in a formation, as if "at a military parade". They are brought to a temporary halt, as the marshland looks "impassable". Here also ended "the last hill of Exmoor", as the stag comes to the end of his territory, his familiar surroundings. As the spectators "high-knee[s]" to a better view, where they can see the hunt with binoculars as if at a favourite sport, while the horsemen look "anxiously" for an alternative route. The hounds put up a cry to scare the stag into a corner, and to direct the hunters.

The stag "drop[s] into a strange country", hearing the sound of hounds behind him. His limbs "cr[y] different directions to his lungs", and he only "want[s] to rest". In unfamiliar territory the progress of the stag will be slow, as he does not know what to expect. He is exhausted by now, as the horsemen "pul[l] aside the camouflage of their terrible planet". The camouflage is of their being civilised, of being anything other than barbarians.

The stag continues desperately, "looking for home", while the countryside opposes him, as "strange trees str[ike] at him and the brambles las[h] him". The empathy of the poet is strongest here, as "the strange earth" and its strange inhabitants, humans, race after him. The thundering in his heart is like "a club beating his ribs", as he escapes for the moment, gets a moment's respite. The crowds of spectators get into their cars and drove away, "wet-through and disappointed", who would have been delighted had the stag been caught.

Hughes brings out the pathos of the plight of the stag, and the cruel brutality of both the spectators and the hunters, as they indulge in the cruel sport of the stag-hunt. His vivid imagery strips away the façade of the humans, their façade of being humane and civilised.

Wind

"Wind" is an autobiographical poem in some ways. Hughes had witnessed a similar storm in a house he was staying in. The poem is additionally symbolic of human relationships, perhaps of Hughes' relationship with his second wife. The poem displays the poet's unusual ability to transform so-called ordinary objects into objects of wonder, as he transports the house "far out at sea all night". The poem describes the far-reaching powerful effects of the storm as compared with the frailty of the humans.

The poem has been written using a traditional quatrain structure. It abounds in rich metaphors and similes, which convey the power of the storm and its effects. Some examples are: "flexing like the lens of a mad eye", "like some fine green goblet". 'Wind' is a descriptive poem, and can be classified as a nature poem. The central interest is the graphic portrayal of the storm and the juxtaposition of humanity and nature.

The poem begins with a strange metaphor – the house being "out at sea all night". Hughes is attempting to convey that the storm raging around the house resembles a sea-storm, both in its duration and intensity. The images and metaphors also portray the same idea – "booming hills", "woods crashing through darkness" and "winds stampeding". The power of the wind is drowning the night.

The wind continues till day break, when a new day "r[ises]". The metaphor here is of relationships, and new dynamics to them. He now has another woman in his life. Just like the landscape is experiencing an external threat, that of the storm, he is experiencing a change in the landscape of his life. The wind throws everything upside down, "flexing like the lens of a mad eye", in the same way the threat of the other woman upsets his relationship with his wife. As the poet is walking or "scaling" the wall along his house, he is plastered against the wall, and he can feel the wind "dent[ing] the balls of [his] eyes". The hills seem weightless like tents, flapping and "strain[ing] the guyrope". The landscape is "quivering", and "the skyline [is] a grimace". It might just disappear any minute. A magpie is flung away by the wind, and the back of a gull "bent like an iron bar".

The entire house seems to shake and ring "like some fine green goblet", going to shatter any moment. Inside it sit the poet and his family, too disturbed for entertainment or talk. The frailty of the house and its occupants are set against the violence of the storm. The poet highlights this by giving most of the space in the poem to the storm, while the humans are huddled into a few lines.

The relationship metaphor is brought out more clearly in the concluding verse. Even though the storm blazes outside the window, like the threat to their relationship, and they can "feel the roots of the house move", they "sit on". Their relationship is shattering, but they do not do anything to prevent it. The outside world is threatening to enter the relationship and wreak havoc, the stones, the very foundations of the house (their relationship) is shaking.

The appeal of the poem lies in its strangely delicate imagery, and the way Hughes combines force at certain times with tremulousness. Also, the metaphor of the house as the relationship is unusual, and catches the reader's interest. "Wind" like his other poems, is unique and stand-alone.

JOHN KEATS

BIOGRAPHY

JOHN KEATS WAS ONE of several children, and came from a fairly poor family in England. Keats lived a short life, but he was remarkably productive, and wrote some of the most beautiful and haunting poetry in the English language during that time. Some of his best poetry, six lyric odes, was written between March and September 1819, at the age of twenty-four. He died just two years later, ending what was surely to be a remarkable literary career.

Keats was born to a lower-middle-class family in 1795 in London. He was the eldest of five children. Whilst he was still a child, he lost both his parents. Keats started a medical apprenticeship at the age of fifteen, but by the age of twenty he left the medical profession to write poems full-time. In 1817, Keats published his first book of poems; however, this was not well-received, receiving harsh criticism from a well-known literary magazine. His second book of poems received even scanter attention.

In 1818, Keats' brother Tom died of tuberculosis, the same disease that claimed his mother, and caused the death of Keats himself a few years later. At this point

Keats moved to Hampstead, where he fell in love with Fanny Brawne. It was during this time that Keats was his most productive. He wrote his best poems, sonnets and lyric odes, in the space of a few years, before his untimely death in 1821. In 1820, he was already quite ill, and moved to sunnier Italy, hoping that his health would take a turn for the better. It was not to be, and Keats died abroad on 23 February 1821. At his request, his tombstone at the Protestant Cemetery in Rome reads: "[h]ere lies one whose name was writ in water".

Keats was heartbroken over the lukewarm reception his work garnered, and he felt that he had made no great contribution in the field of poetry in his lifetime. Even his friends were disappointed and angered on his behalf, adding the following lines to his epitaph: "This Grave / contains all that was Mortal / of a young English Poet / who, / on his Death Bed, in the Bitterness of his Heart / at the Malicious Power of his Enemies / Desired / these Words to be engraven on his Tomb Stone..."

At the time of Keats' death, he had been writing poetry seriously for about six years, and publishing for about four. He had sold barely 200 copies of his poetry in his lifetime, and received almost no public praise. However, his work shows remarkable maturity and complexity, extraordinary for someone who had only been working as a poet for a very short time. His poems were full of beauty, packed full with sensuous imagery and allegory. His most famous poems are his odes, written in a few short months, not long after the death of his brother. Perhaps the circumstances of Keats' life, having lost his parents and then his brother, watching them die painful deaths, contributed to his sensitivity and maturity as a poet, and infused his words with lyrical magic. The poet who, in life did not receive much recognition, became immortal in death, and remains one of the most studied and most loved poets of all time.

CRITICAL ANALYSIS OF SELECTED POEMS

On First Looking Into Chapman's Homer

John Keats loved reading classical literature, and having read Chapman's translation of Homer, a profound change overcame him. The epic had such a hold over him, he felt compelled to write this poem. The poem, "On First Looking into Chapman's Homer", talks of Keats' ecstasy and sense of mystery and wonderment on reading the works of Homer. The language used in the poem is Shakespearean English, and it is in the form of a Petrarchan sonnet.

The poet begins with the rich imagery of classical literature – "realms of gold". It introduces the central theme of the poem, namely, reading a new and unknown great poem is like discovering "goodly states and kingdoms". He says that he has traversed many lands, and seen many poets in loyal service to Apollo. He has often heard of a rich and beautiful region ruled by Homer – that of poetry and literature – but he has never experienced it himself. Here Keats expresses his fascination for the classical Greek world and attempts to express a philosophy through classical legend.

The poet then writes that his vision and sense were awakened once he had first read Chapman's translation of Homer's epics. To him it feels like the discovery of a new planet or star by an astronomer, or the discovery of the Pacific by the Spanish explorer Cortez as he gazed at it from a mountain peak up in the Gulf of Darien with his men. The imagery and feel of the poem is the culmination of Keats' poetic genius, as he describes his feelings with phrases like "with eagle eyes" and "a wild sunrise".

The poem brings out Keats' love for classical literature and Greek legend. Though rich imagery and beauty of sound he expresses his deep feelings to the reader.

Last Sonnet

John Keats wrote some of the most beautiful and enduring poems in the English language. In his short life span, and even shorter period of writing, he wrote a sequence of six lyrical odes and several other sonnets and poems. Keats' family was quite poor and he lost many of his family members to diseases like tuberculosis, of which he himself died. The realisation of his mortality gave a lot of depth to many of his lyrics. This is also the motivation behind this poem, "Last Sonnet", where he faces the possibility of death and feels that he wants to experience life to its fullest before dying.

The poem is a sonnet, as its name suggests, it is in fact his last sonnet. Its rhyme-scheme is *ABABCDCDEFEFGG*. In this respect, it is a

Shakespearean sonnet, consisting of three quatrains and a couplet.

The poem commences with the poet's wish to remain as steadfast as the star shining brightly in the heavens, yet he does not want to remain alone up there. "With eternal lids apart" is a metaphor for steadfastness, illustrating how the star shines on, without even blinking. The poet further compares the star to a hermit.

It seems to the poet that the oceans are carrying out a "priest-like task" – a metaphor for the ceremonial cleansing of the shores. The star watches this, as it watches the newly-fallen snow on the mountains and the moor; without judgement, without comment. The poet does not want to be like the star, silently watching; he wants to experience life on his own.

The poet goes on to write that he wants to make love to a beautiful woman, and lie on her breast and feel her breath. Here Keats has created a metaphor for life, telling us how he wants to live life fully, experience its pulse, experience each moment. He would not mind lying awake all night, or being still, as long as he can suck the most out of life. He would rather die than live life half-heartedly, or live for the sake of being alive.

Keats wrote this poem when he was facing the fact that he was to die shortly. At the time, he must have felt that even though he did not have long to live, he would like to live it fully and enjoy every minute of it. Using rich metaphors throughout the poem – that of the star, the priest, the ocean and the woman – the poet has explained himself and his state of mind eloquently. The poem seems to go to the heart of Keats' emotions, and that to me is the most appealing aspect of this particular poem.

La Belle Dame Sans Merci

Keats talks of poetry and poetic inspiration in this poem. It describes beautifully the poetic semicircle of imaginative ascent, fulfilment and descent back into the world of reality. There are recurrent metaphors describing the poetic process, in a ballad form, symbolically narrating the poetic experience.

The poem begins and ends with a stark picture of a dying season. The sedge has withered and no birds are singing. The troubled knight is experiencing pain. He has been lured into the desolate maize of reality, a hell where nature mirrors the desolation experienced by the knight, who can also be identified as a poet. The images are of an autumn season – "granary is full...harvest's done".

The knight is a youthful wayfarer on a quest, an altruist who hopes to serve humanity. Unfortunately, the knight seems to have forsworn his duty as he falls under the spell of the beautiful lady without pity, "la belle dame sans merci". He is merely a courtier, who loves this lady, without any hope of her returning or reciprocating that love.

The knight describes how he reached the state portrayed by him in the previous lines. The lady he meets enthrals him, and he gets swept away by her beauty. Her "wild eyes" and long hair are associated with imaginative inspiration and vision. The knight is drawn to her by her beauty and her songs. The "sets" symbolises that once it has been regularised by the poet, the imagination sets forth. At this, the prince is charmed. The weaving of garlands symbolises the poem he weaves. The knight wants to bind and hold his imagination, trying to achieve a permanence of poetic intensity. Yet he fails, as the lady plants within him the roots of music – "relish sweet" and "manna-dew" of inspiration. These are going to grow into poetry.

The knight is raised to passionate heights of imaginative inspiration at her confession of love, and is allowed admission into her "elfin grot", symbolising entry into the sanctuary of poetry and imagination. Yet, during their lovemaking, she realises the futility of it, as it is sure to come to an end.

Then, the knight is abruptly placed "on the cold hill side", heralding the death of imagination and the oncoming pain at the return to reality. The beautiful lady, having nourished the poet and fulfilled his hunger for poetic vision, mercilessly withdraws her favours, starving and destroying those who earn their nourishment from the pursuit of poetry. The knight does not understand the risks involved in trying to bind momentous and fleeting bouts of imagination. The inevitable waning of imagination leaves him sapped of strength and vitality. He "sojourns" on the cold hillside, "alone and palely loitering", without muse or music. He roams, hoping that he may find his beautiful lady and experience another temporary, but exquisite love-dream. Just as there is the end of a season, of a life and of a dream, Keats suggests that the imagination too has its inevitable and natural decline. Just as it ascends you to an enthralling peak, it drops you to an unbelievable canyon, leaving you much worse and more desolate than before.

To Autumn

Keats was a brilliant poet, and even though his career lasted only a few year, his productivity was prodigious. He lost many of his family members, and ultimately died himself, at a young age, of tuberculosis. This ode, 'To Autumn', is written as an acceptance of his impending death. Keats wrote this poem in 1820. Autumn signifies the coming of the end of the year, and of life. Therefore by accepting, even celebrating, autumn in the poem, Keats reveals his acceptance and coming to terms with the end of his own life.

The poem 'To Autumn' is a three-stanza ode. Each stanza is eleven lines long, with a varying rhyme scheme, and each verse begins with an *ABAB* rhyme scheme. The remaining seven lines have alternate rhyme patterns.

The poem is set during the season of autumn. Autumn is personified in this poem – "season of mists". The fruit trees are loaded with fruit, bending under the load of its burden. Autumn is plotting, along with the sun, how to bless the vines, so they grow more bountifully. Autumn "swells the gourd" and "plumps the hazel shells". Autumn will ripen the flowers now, so that they produce seeds to produce flowers for the bees next year. This signifies the continuance of the cycle of life – life and death – and how one is essential for the other. The sense is one of warmth, maturity and ripeness. The days are full of warmth, summer seems to overflow.

The poet then personifies Autumn as a woman. She is often reported to be seen amongst her store of goodies, where the stocks for winter have been stored, "sitting careless on a granary floor". Her hair is "soft-lifted" by the wind, and she sleeps in the fields. In the first instance Autumn is personified as a harvester. In the second image Autumn is personified as a reaper. It is a drowsy and happy image. As the reaper falls asleep for a moment, the next few plants get a respite; it signifies the cutting down of nature to give way to winter. Autumn in the next instant is personified as a gleaner, gleaning the remnants of nature and beauty from the surrounding world. Here, the poet is gleaning wisdom by accepting the passage of time, the changing of the seasons and the cycle of life. The last personification is that of a farmer watching his cider-press squeezing the juice from apples, signifying the poet's desire to squeeze every ounce of joy and life from his last few moments left on earth.

The poet asks about the lost beauty, youth and life that spring has taken with it. Now all that remains are the "stubble-plains", imparting a rosy hue to the land. Gnats are lifted and dropped by the breeze amongst the river willows. Lambs born in spring are now full-grown to face the winter, and are bleating loudly. Birds are twittering in the skies, getting ready to migrate for the winter. The scene expresses calm and serenity, it exudes a positive air.

In this poem, Keats pays homage to Autumn – a time of warmth and plenty, but perched on the edge of winter's desolation. The mood of the entire ode is calm and serene, unlike that in "Ode to a Nightingale", one of Keats' other famous odes. This poem offers a solution rather than posing a question. It is flawlessly constructed, and thematically expresses harmony with nature. The poem does not exhibit any strong emotions; the reader does not feel the poet's anguish as deeply as in some of his other poems. He reveals acceptance of the cycle of life and nature, and shows a simple appreciation of beauty through simple, yet powerful images. The most stirring aspect of the poem is its simplicity, yet lasting impact, and the realisation that appreciation of all that is good and beautiful need not stop just because one life is ending, because another is beginning elsewhere.

PHILIP LARKIN

BIOGRAPHY OF PHILIP LARKIN

PHILIP ARTHUR LARKIN WAS born in 1922 in Coventry, Warwickshire. Larkin attended school in Coventry, and wrote for *The Coventrian*, his school magazine. He went to St. John's College, Oxford in 1940, and graduated First Class Honours in English in 1943. Larkin failed the army medical due to his poor eyesight, and was able to complete his education without interruption.

Larkin was influenced by contemporaries Auden, Yeats and Lawrence, as well as university friends like Kingsley Amis. He published his first poem in November 1940. Failing to enter the Civil Service, Larkin became a librarian in Wellington, Shropshire in 1943. In 1946, he became assistant librarian at the University College, Leicester. He moved to Queen's University, Belfast in 1950, and took up his final post as University Librarian at the University of Hull, where he remained till his death. During this time, he continued to write and published his first book of poems, *The North Ship* in 1945. His first novel *Jill* was published a year later. These were not well-received, but his next novel, *A Girl in Winter*, was well-received when it was published by Faber and Faber in 1947.

Larkin's next volume of poems, *The Less Deceived* (1955), was written in Belfast, and this volume really established his credence as a poet. After the publication of *The Whitsun Weddings* in 1964, he was honoured with a Fellowship of the Royal Society of Literature. He was also awarded the Queen's Gold Medal for Poetry. In the next few years Larkin wrote his most famous poems, including 'The Building', which were published in his last collection in 1974, *High Windows*. In 1975, he received the CBE.

After this, Larkin all but stopped writing poetry, although *Required Writing: Miscellaneous Pieces 1955-1982* was published in 1983, and won the W.H. Smith Literary Award the next year. He also received several honorary doctorates, including one from Oxford University. He declined the offer to be named Poet Laureate, and was detected with cancer of the oesophagus in 1985. He died on 2 December 1985, aged 63.

Philip Larkin was different from other literary figures, mostly keeping to himself. He had a string of relationships, and was not always monogamous. Some of Larkin's most amusing and interesting poems deal with the different facets of human beings when they are in relationships. Not only do his poems illuminate human nature, they reveal Larkin's acerbic sense of humour and his outlook on the world. Whilst he himself shunned publicity and media attention, preferring to live a quiet, academic life, his writings earned him numerous accolades as well as cemented his position as one of the notable poets of the twentieth century.

CRITICAL ANALYSIS OF SELECTED POEMS

Poetry Of Departures

In this poem, 'Poetry of Departures', Philip Larkin is satirising the appeal of the wanderlust in the poet, showing its attraction and the longing for immediacy and action. The poem contains a debate between two opposing points of view, and like most of his other work, it is more intellectual than emotional. At first, the idea of leaving home sounds very attractive, but the poet then comes to the conclusion that such a life would have something artificial about it.

The poem is written in a colloquial, conversational style, characteristic of Larkin. It displays Larkin's laconic manner of expressing himself, and is a model of compression and condescension. Often syntax is sacrificed for the sake of economy, and even the stanza is not seen as a complete unit in itself. Many of the stanzas are enjambed, and echo the "audacious" action by portraying an "audacious" style of writing.

The poem opens very casually, without a definite resolve in the poet's mind. The title itself suggests that there is something poetic or alluring about leaving home to lead a life of travel and adventure. The casual "fifth-hand" report and interspersion of "I" and "we" makes the poem sound inter-personal. Though the poet portrays the man's move as heroic, ironically, he uses the word "epitaph", perhaps signifying the death of his soul. He says that the person reporting sounds as if he is "certain you approve" the rebellious action, "elemental" as it lets you be who you are, and "purifying" because one is getting rid of superfluous things, and leading the life he wants to lead. Larkin is being ironic and sarcastic here.

The poet says in a familiar way that "we all hate home". He is speaking of the impulse to rebel, and that it is perfectly justified to want to rebel. "Home" here is a metaphor for the present existence he is living. The "junk" signifies the accumulated, "specially-chosen" mementos collected over time. The poet says that what he dislikes most is when everything is in place, all the necessary requirements for a good life are present, "my life is in perfect order"; yet that order is what restricts his freedom, and lends to the sense of being superficial. The essence of the sentiment is that when you lead a life that you are supposed to lead, then you end up wanting to rebel.

The poet then describes a move of finality, "[h]e walked out on the whole crowd", yet at the same time remains prudent and sensible of the difficulties involved – "I'd go today…if it wasn't so artificial". He describes instances related to violence and pleasure that would arouse him, and says that since he knows that he can leave anytime, paradoxically, it helps him stay "sober and industrious".

Larkin is agreeable to lead this Bohemian life, travelling, encountering adventure, "crouch in the fo'c'sle", if he knew that it wasn't a step backward. The juxtaposition of the rough and smooth images brings home the fact with a shock, that even rebelling from conformity is another form of conforming, as one is following someone else's beliefs of freedom, not one's own. He says that it is "a deliberate step backwards" for civilisation, represented by books, as they provide knowledge. The poet mentions china, by which he refers to delicate, superficial aspects of life. They create a life "reprehensibly perfect", but not really. In leaving everything behind, instead of a step forward, it is backward; similarly a step backward for civilisation. Just as the previous life is artificial and mapped, so is this as it too is mapped.

This poem is a parody of the poet's own emotional excitement arising out of thoughts of being a rebel, and chalks out his dissatisfaction as a set of stark choices. It contrasts a wild, romantic impulse with a conservative, cautious one. The tone of the poem is robustly comic and confident, and dramatizes everyday life erroneously. Though the poet sets out by arguing out both sides equally, he ends with the finality of a decision, stating that whatever the constraints, rebelling is just as much conforming as staying in the same pattern of life.

The Building

Larkin wrote the poem "The Building" from his own experiences. The poem describes a hospital, the people that come in to the hospital and the activities inside.

The building is high, and its "lucent comb" is glimmering for all to see. Around it the streets seem to be sighing, as they "rise and fall". Cars continuously drawing up in front of it "are not taxis"; they are ambulances, bringing patients to the hospital. All around pervades a "frightening smell", the smell of fear, and of death.

Larkin describes the scene as you enter the building, the hospital. There are people reading paperbacks, and drinking cups of tea, giving the appearance of an airport lounge. People "tamely sit", there is no excitement. The scene is reminiscent of daily routine. Mostly everyone is in outdoor clothes, some just returned from shopping, or having brought along things they might need. Faces are "restless and resigned", as if knowing that the wait is long, or that they are resigned to their fate.

When a nurse appears, people get up expectantly, hoping to be called. As someone is taken away, the rest return to his or her occupations. While getting up, one drops things, and so you sit down, searching for "dropped gloves or cards". This is symbolic of life, when people go through it expecting every moment that something important will happen to them, and until then they keep waiting, spending their time in idle pursuits. Homes and names in the hospital are in "abeyance"; where everyone is in neutral ground. Anyone and everyone can come there. This is symbolic of the fact that however much money or wealth one may possess, one cannot buy human life, or happiness of a lasting kind. Mostly everyone in the hospital is there without a choice, for them the hospital represents the last hope they have.

The poet says that everyone is there to "confess", to treat a complaint. The word "confess" can also symbolize religious confession, signifying that this is when people turn to God. The poet states that there must be a terrible "error" that such a building needs so many floors, and so much money is used in the building and infrastructure. The people there have stopped their daily routine to be there on a working day, moving from floor to floor. On the way, they glance at each other, trying to guess what each person's ailment might be. "Someone's wheeled past", someone who is obviously now dead. The people around are "quiet"; they suddenly realize their own mortality, a "new thing held in common".

The further one retreats inside the hospital, the more difficult it is "to return from". The contrast between the outside and the inside of the building is emphasized. Everything "seems old enough", or normal enough outside; children playing, people driving, traffic; while inside there is uncertainty. The "locked church" may signify the fact that even religion will not help them now; the hospital truly is their last hope.

The people are haunted by the fact that they may not leave alive, while the outside world continues in a feeling of normalcy. What is going on in the world, what everyone takes for granted, is out of reach for those who are going to die. Mortality is unreal for most people, but at some point one becomes aware of it.

"A touching dream to which we all are lulled

But wake from separately".

One tries to protect oneself from accepting reality, however the illusion "collapses" once inside these corridors.

Each person goes inside, but they will leave at different times. Some are not in immediate danger, and "will be out by lunch, or four"; while others may never leave. They would join "the unseen congregations", also referring to religion. Everyone's diverse paths lead to the same destination – death.

"This place accepts" this fact, and so do the others eventually. They will all die someday, maybe now, maybe later. A person would be really lucky not to die in a hospital, in this "clean-sliced cliff". People turn to religion, which might extend life, or help you come to terms with death, but never escape it. However, relentlessly people keep trying to offer "propitiatory flowers" to God, hoping to make themselves less mortal.

The poem brings out the glaring reality experienced in a hospital, yet one that all of us have to face at some time or the other. It also symbolizes the hospital as a place of hope, the last resort of the sick and dying. Larkin, in this poem, engages the reader in the most fundamental question of all, that of life and death, and how to deal with it.

Wild Oats

Larkin has often been criticised for writing mostly of gloomy, depressing subjects. Others feel however, that his poetry should be lauded as honestly portraying various aspects of life in England. This poem, "Wild Oats" is an instance where Larkin describes the battle between conditioning and reality in a relationship. His colloquial, easy style conveys his point more effectively than any other.

The phrase, to sow one's 'wild oats', refers to someone having a number of sexual relationships, all of them casual. The poem opens with a scene at the poet's workplace, most probably a library, as he worked in several. Two girls came in, one was a beautiful "bosomy....rose", while the other one was wearing spectacles, an intelligent girl. This is where the battle in Larkin's mind begins. "Shooting-match" refers to the relationship, as the poet says that in those times beauty was sufficient for a relationship, and the first girl was exceedingly pretty, a typical English rose. Yet for the moment, conditioning won, as he "took out" the friend, reason being, though there existed no chemistry between the two, at least he could talk to her.

The poet describes their relationship as being a very communicative one, in seven years they "wrote over four hundred letters". He gave her "a ten guinea-ring", which was restored to him when the relationship ended. They met "at numerous cathedral cities". He confesses that he met "beautiful" twice. He thinks that she never found him attractive, and possibly "was trying...not to laugh".

Larkin tried to make a long-term relationship with "the friend", yet after five live-ins, they mutually gave up. She called him "too selfish, withdrawn / and easily bored to love", which remark he brushed off as a useful thing to know. All these years later, Larkin still has two snaps "of bosomy rose with fur gloves on", a reminder to him of what he gave up. He terms the photographs as "unlucky charms", as they could have been the cause for the relationship with the friend not working. He obviously still lusted after "bosomy rose", at a gut level always knowing that she was the one he actually felt attracted to.

This poem is about the choice between what we want and what we think we should have, the choice between the possible and the impossible, the choice between what our heart desires and what our head tells us to pursue. In this poem, Larkin shows us that he can veer away from his usual serious prose and write humorous, sarcastic verse as well.

Church Going

This poem is, in Larkin's own words, about "going to church, not religion." In Larkin's usual style, the poem is of a cynical nature, and there is a strong current of scepticism running through it. The poem expresses doubts about the validity of atheism either as a creed or as an attitude.

It has been written in seven stanzas of nine lines each. The rhyme scheme is *ABABCADCD*. The midway path between following an accepted and traditional rhyme scheme, and not having one at all has been achieved by him; and this characterises his views on the subject, of following a middle path between blind faith and atheism. The diction consists mainly of words with religious annotations, however, rather than conveying veneration, they are suggestive of irreverence.

The poet enters the church, making sure no mass or sermon is going on. The church is inert. He shuts the door with a "thud", shutting the world out, and making sure he isn't disturbed. He notices the decorations and details, listing them out, as this is just "another church". The beauty of the church doesn't strike him; he only lists the details like a detached observer. Flowers in the room have begun to wither, perhaps as a symbol for the withering influence of religion, or his withering atheism. The silence is overpowering, pregnant with the absence of voices, absence perhaps of a realisation. According to him, it has been "brewing" for a considerable time -- maybe alluding to the brewing discord and dissatisfaction with religion taking place in the world. The poet seems to feel a whimsical sort of respect, even though there is nothing noteworthy about the church, and thus "take[s] off" his cycle-clips "in awkward reverence".

Larkin moves ahead and explores the various corners of the church, commenting on the restorative cleanliness of the church in a mocking tone. He preaches "here endeth" in an irreligious, emotionless way. The irony of these words is linked to the poem's title, in a way reflecting the possibility of the church's redundancy. They may also, in paradox, suggest that his sojourn to the church is not yet over. The reference to Ireland relates to their deep religious nature, and may also be a reference to Yeats, who was an early influence on Larkin. Yeats' emphasis on ritualistic ceremonies is significant here.

We now find out that the poet often stops by churches, often as a compulsion, he rather enjoys it. His reasons do not stem from any religious faith, rather they could stem from a quest, a misty quest of which he is not very clear, and his purpose still seems hazy. Each time he admits to being similarly frustrated, yet he keeps returning, perhaps yearning for a visionary moment, but he remains unenlightened. Though churches have no traditional significance to him, he feels that there ought to be something of purport to the whole thing; an issue over which great wars were fought, an issue that seems to be such a significant and important part of many people's lives. There is undoubtedly something that he is missing, and he longs to understand what it is.

As Larkin plumbs the depths of his metaphysical speculations, he wonders increasingly about churches, and their significance in people's lives many years from that moment. Will churches still be in use then? If not, what will replace it? In addition, what will the churches (temples / mosques) be converted to? Will they be utilised as museums "chronically on show", or will nature be allowed to run its course? Will superstition be abandoned along with religion, or will they be termed "unlucky"? This sense of wonder characterises the poem, and supports the notion of the poet's amazement at the incommunicable yearning he feels at churches.

Larkin here expresses his belief that someday religion will not be needed, as it is a man-made institution, and like all man-made institutions, will perish away. He asks what will happen when that takes place. Will then "dubious women", full of superstition and residual religiosity bring their children to touch the altar and get blessed? Alternatively, will remedies for cancer be found there, growing among the ruins? Religion, even in its absence, gives power to some, and takes it away from others. The power game will continue to be played long after religion is outdated. He then questions what will remain when disbelief has gone. The existence of belief has to be acknowledged to disbelieve it. At this point all that remains is nature, as it takes over everything. His scepticism here deflects his wonder, and the possibility for a visionary moment appears improbable.

He then wonders who the last people to visit churches will be. Will they be ecclesiastical anthropologists, antique collectors or "Christmas-addict[s]" who will strip the church of its now forgotten religious dignity? As the days pass by, the original significance of it will diminish, and those remaining will remember less of what it originally stood for. The place would most likely be frequented by collectors of religious souvenirs, "one of the crew", rather than genuinely reverent people.

He also feels that people like him could also visit the place -- "bored, uniformed"; though believing that even the residue of religion has vaporised, but attracted there on the strength of what it once represented and affirmed, at least on the ceremonial level -- "marriage. And birth, and death". Now that religion has fallen apart, these things are not together anymore. The poet demonstrates a longing for its ritual integrity, its past vitality. Churches are important, because they bring into focus the bearing of ethics, philosophy and history upon human nature. He feels that though he is unable to fully comprehend the worth of this institution, he is glad to "stand in silence" there.

Larkin mocks the seriousness of people, as they make religion a "serious" business. The air is "blent" of all things we feel to have worth, and they are garbed as our destinies. He also plays on the way religion preaches certain doctrines, displaying a tendency to be dogmatic. He says that the desire of the human is to "be more serious", always find something to worship, to revere, and that this nature will never change, even though its object might.

Reasons For Attendance

Larkin himself was never in too many long term relationships, thus in this poem, one interpretation could be that he is defending his "reasons for [not] attend[ing]". He is questioning the concept that happiness can only be achieved as one half of a couple, and elucidates reasons one should or should not be in a love relationship. The poem is characteristically in Larkin's style, colloquial and informal, and takes the form of an ongoing debate in the poet's mind, and instead of definitely resolving the debate, Larkin leaves the choice of whether to be in a relationship to each individual.

The poem opens with a dance, as the trumpet plays. The atmosphere is flushed, heated, as couples dance "on the beat of happiness". The dancing couples, "all under twenty-five", are a metaphor for a love relationship, while the "lighted glass" signifies the barrier between those watching the dancers and those dancing. It is clear that the debate is between the watchers and the doers. The poet is content to be a watcher, as he has learnt his lesson and does not want to repeat his follies. He comments that, to the couples, the pursuit of happiness is a solemn one.

The poet "sens[es]" the atmosphere, almost as if he cannot directly hear or see, due to the fact that his viewpoint is vastly different. He poses two questions that go straight to the crux of the subject – "why be out here?" and "why be in there?" He says that the advantages are "sex", but is that enough? He challenges the notion that only couples find "the lion's share of happiness", and reiterates that he does not need to be in love to be happy. What the poet is really questioning is why do people need to have relationships? Is a relationship a guarantee of love and happiness? Or is it possible to be happy even without being in a romantic relationship? These are universal questions, ones that we ask every time we find ourselves freshly single or are asked pointed questions about our lack of a relationship. Especially in today's age, when long term relationships are no longer required for either sex or companionship, one often wonders whether it still is the only way.

The Whitsun Weddings

This poem is the title poem from the collection "The Whitsun Weddings". Whitsunday is the festival celebrating the descent of the Holy Spirit upon the

Apostles. It is so called because of the tradition of wearing white clothes on that day, and it is the seventh Sunday after Easter. It is observed by feasting, and the day is also a favourite for baptism and joining the church. A subtle allusion could also be to the "wit" that the Holy Spirit bestows to worshippers (wisdom). Marriage carries sacramental associations as the church sanctions the pact between two people. The poem explores how marriage can be seen as both fettering and freeing.

The poem commences in a casual tone as a detached rail traveller comments on his experiences during the journey. The weather is sunny, and as the train passes houses, a street, the smelly "fish-docks", it seems as though they are travelling along the horizon.

Then a description of the journey follows -- it is nearly noon, as the sun is making "short-shadow[s]". The traveller describes the scenery with great attention to detail -- "canals with floating of industrial froth", hedges, farms. Mostly he can smell the "reek" of the "carriage-cloth", but occasionally the smell of fresh grass overpowers him. The passing towns do not stand out, they are "new and nondescript", and the train approaches "acres of dismantled cars" as they pass junkyards along the way.

Hearing the noise outside on the station, he first thinks that it is porters "larking with the mails", and he goes on reading. At some point, he begins to notice the "grinning and pomaded girls", with their "whoops and skirls". Almost caricatures, with "heels and veils", the girls self-consciously watch them go by. He seems to be mocking these girls, who are grossly overdressed and stand out amidst the drab surroundings.

It seems to the traveller that they are "waving goodbye", as the sole survivor of marriage. He begins to observe more closely now; some girls are conspicuous because of their clothes, while fathers, mothers, uncles are all standing about shouting advice, and generally creating a ruckus. He is mocking the institution of marriage, and commenting on the loud, garish passers-by. As the couples prepare for their departures, the expressions on each face reveal their thoughts. Children find the whole occasion "dull", while fathers consider it a waste of money and "farcical", and girls, "gripping their handbags tighter", fear their turn. Here a patriarchal view of marriage is being displayed, where women are the ones to perpetuate the institution of marriage. Freedom here is in a way being curtailed, as the woman enters wedlock, incumbent with responsibility, fear and emotions. However, it can also be freeing as one is now free of superficiality and plasticity.

The train moves towards London, expelling "gouts of steam". In a short space of time, the traveller has seen a "dozen marriages got under way". There is a juxtaposition of light and grave feelings -- with the image of "[s]ettling hats", and saying "I nearly died". The superficial one is denigrating the serious image, also making the reader wonder why. Within this time, twenty-four people have committed to each other for a lifetime; however, they are unconcerned of anything or anyone around.

As he nears London, the traveller meditates on this "travelling coincidence". The train journey could be interpreted as a metaphor for married life. It is a change in one's life. Happiness in marriage is a matter of chance. One shoots an arrow into the future, but does not know where it could land. Successful marriages are those in which the partners adjust - "change" according to one another. There is also a reference to Cupid's "arrow[s]" here. The poet, as the traveller, regards marriage as an enduring rather than decaying institution, and does not write it off, rather, ends on a note of hope.

Dockery and Son

The poem "Dockery and Son" is about self-analysis and a journey inside the poet's soul, assessing the course of his life. He realises that his life has passed him by, and he is wondering whether it has gone the way he would have wanted it to.

The first half of the poem constitutes a witty and well-observed narrative, but this is only a backdrop for the later, more reflective stanzas. The poet is conversing with his college dean, and their dialogue captures their mutual insincerity and artifice. The dean informs the poet that his old classmate Dockery's son is now studying in that school. Memories of his school life come back to him, but he finds that the door to his past is "locked"; he can't enter that phase of his life again.

In contrast with the gloomy corridors, the outside is beautiful and dazzling. The poet is "ignored", because he has not sent an heir back to the school. He feels a familiar sense of distance and disappointment. The chance comment "his son's here now" shocks him into reflection, as he realises that the son must have been born when his friend was twenty. How would the father of the boy, who "must have been born in '43", have made such important decisions at such a young age? He reflects on Dockery, not even remembering completely who he was. He associates him with a dead roommate, and remembers that he was "withdrawn". It occurs to him that one never knows "how much [or] how little" one knows of a person. To the poet, Dockery must have been the boy most unlikely to have a child and settle down at twenty.

The poet falls asleep, awakening at "the fumes and furnace glares" of Sheffield. The "joining and parting" lines illustrate the meeting and parting between lovers, while the moon symbolizes romantic love. The moon's reflection is symbolic of his own reflections, that of a life empty of those things that to others "seemed quite natural" – a wife, a son, a home. He has none of these, and neither does he seem to want them. Yet he reflects on the fact that his wants are different, he only feels a sense of "numbness". The poet realises that a lot of life has "gone" by, and "how widely from the others". He wonders that Dockery, "only nineteen", was capable of deciding what he wanted and "taking stock" of his life.

However, the difference between them was Dockery's conviction that he wanted a child. This is contrasted with the attitude of the poet to having children; to him it meant "dilution", a lessening of his self. He is asking himself why people don't stop to question these "innate assumptions". He observes that these "assumptions" don't come from people's deepest beliefs, instead according to him, they stem from their warped, narrow minds. They are then left with the things they are imposed with, and these expectations become a habit.

When the poet looks back at his previous beliefs and thoughts, the past "rear[s] like sand-clouds", and seems to choke him. The "sand-clouds" embody a son for Dockery, but for him "nothing". His son looks after him, "patron[ises]" him by not being born. The poet feels that life could initially be boring, as maybe he is leading someone else's life. Then it turns to "fear", as he realises that life is passing one by. Life passes by regardless of whether it is lived to the full or not. It leaves something behind, even though we do not immediately realise what it is. The poet realises that others' lives are completely different, and wonders, and attributes something to it. He wonders whether this is what Dockery wanted. He looks back at his own life, and wonders where it went. Is this what he wanted? All that is left is "what something hidden from us chose", and old age, and eventually death.

In this poem, prompted by a chance comment, Larkin looks back at the life he has led, and wonders whether this is what he really wanted. The poem can be seen as an expression of midlife crisis, where the poet is at a point in his life where the road ahead of him forks in two directions, and he has to make a decision of which road to take. Moreover, this is a chance for him to reconsider the path he has chosen thus far, and how he views this path. Will he continue as before, or will this comment cause him to change his behaviour going forward? Will he be swayed by society's "innate assumptions" or continue to forge his own path?

W. B. YEATS

BIOGRAPHY OF W. B. YEATS

WILLIAM BUTLER YEATS WAS an Irish poet and dramatist, and widely regarded as one of the best poets of the 20th century. He was born in 1865 in Dublin, Ireland. Yeats hailed from an artistic family; his father was a portrait painter, his brother became a renowned painter and his sisters were involved in the Arts and Crafts movement. They moved to London when Yeats was two, and he shuttled between County Sligo, Ireland and London for most of his childhood. He regarded County Sligo, where his maternal external family lived, as very close to his heart.

Yeats' family came from a Protestant background, and sympathized with the changes in Irish politics, but the contrast between his Protestant past and the Roman Catholic background of Ireland led him to spiritual confusion and exploration of theological subjects. He studied spiritualism, mysticism, Hinduism and the Kabbalah, in an attempt to make sense of the confusion he felt. He also read the works of Shakespeare, William Blake, Dante Alighieri, and John Donne to fuel his own prose. Yeats' education was sporadic, partly homeschooled, and partly attending various schools where he was an average student.

In 1881, the family moved back to Dublin, where William attended high school and spent a lot of time at his fathers' studio, and in the company of artists and writers. He first started writing poetry at this time, and in 1885, some of his work appeared in the *Dublin University Review*, whilst he was enrolled at the Metropolitan School of Art. Yeats' early work was heavily influenced by Percy Shelley, Edmund Spenser and pre-Raphaelite verse, but later turned towards Irish myth and lore, and the work of William Blake, an English poet whose work was characterized by religious and spiritual symbolism. He was also greatly influenced by the occult, the magical and the mystical, dabbling in Eastern and Western religious and spiritual tradition, which manifested in many of his most famous work.

Throughout a large part of Yeats' life, he was in love with a woman named Maud Gonne, who did not reciprocate his feelings. Yeats met Maud Gonne, who was an Irish patriot and revolutionary in 1889. He fell in love with her almost immediately, and remained in love with her all his life, despite her numerous rejections. She became his muse, almost haunting him, and Yeats wrote several poems about her or alluding to her.

Yeats helped found the Abbey Theatre, one of Ireland's most important cultural institutions. He was elected to the Irish Senate in 1922, where he served for six years. Yeats was awarded the Nobel Prize for Literature in 1923. Although Yeats had been writing poetry from a young age, it was only in his 50s that he became one of the best poets writing in the English language. In fact, he wrote his best poems after receiving the Nobel Prize.

Yeats died at the age of seventy-three on 28 January 1939. He was at first buried in Roquebrune-Cap-Martin, France, and later, according to his wishes, re-interred in 1948 at County Sligo, Ireland. His gravestone is inscribed with the words from one of his poems: "Cast a cold Eye, / On Life, / On Death. / Horseman, pass by!"

CRITICAL ANALYSIS OF SELECTED POEMS

He Wishes For The Cloths Of Heaven

Yeats loved a woman named Maud Gonne for over 20 years, but his love for her was unrequited. She was an activist in Ireland, and went on to marry someone else, a fellow activist. Yeats however, never gave up loving her, and wrote many love-poems, probably inspired by her. This poem, "He Wishes for the Cloths of Heaven", encapsulates his strength of devotion in a beautiful way, as he moves away from elaboration to simplicity.

The rhythm of the poem is like a chant forced by the adjectives and repetitions, and creates an incantatory quality. The richly colourful adjectives add to the mystery of the poem. There is a wishful tone of longing and the fulfilment of love.

Yeats says that if he had all the "heavens' embroidered cloths", worked with "golden and silver light", he would lay them under her, his lover's, feet. He would bring cloths that were representative of day, twilight and night, with all possible hues and richness. However, he laments, that he is poor, and has "only [his] dreams". These he can gladly give her, and has spread his dreams under her feet. His love for her can express itself only by his gift of his most precious possessions, his dreams. He thus exhorts her to be gentle, to tread softly, as she "tread[s] on [his] dreams", as he opens up his heart to her.

This poem is beautiful, and stands out in its exquisite imagery and sheer simplicity. His heartfelt rendition of his love, and the way he opens up his heart, makes this one of his most beautiful and memorable love-poems.

Song Of Wandering Aengus

Aengus in Celtic mythology is the god of youth, beauty, poetry and love. There are many legends associated with him. One legend states that Aengus' kisses were supposed to have been transformed into birds which flew constantly about his head. Yeats uses the legend of Aengus to express his futile love for the woman he loved for twenty years, Maud Gonne, and his undaunted quest for her love.

Aengus, who has caught at dawn a "little silver trout" on his hazelwand, finds it transformed into a "glimmering girl with apple blossom in her hair". Fish here could symbolize the poetic inspiration or Maud Gonne, and he is describing his quest for either. The girl then calls him by his name, and then runs away through "the brightening air".

The poet then says that though he is old, and has wandered through hills and vales in his futile quest, he is determined to find her. He dreams of kissing her hands, walking through grassy meadows, plucking "silver apples of the moon", and "golden apples of the sun".

There are several ways of interpreting the poem. Firstly, it is interesting to note that Yeats had first seen Maud Gonne standing beside a bouquet of apple blossoms, and thereafter he always associated her complexion with apple blossoms. The silver and golden apples are symbols from Kabbalistic lore of fruits from the Tree of Life -- feminine and masculine. Yeats was very interested in and influenced by Kabbalistic teachings.

Another way to read the poem is to treat it as an embodiment of one of the legends about the women of Sidhe, who in Irish folklore were believed to be people from the Faery Hills, and who disguised themselves as fishes to bewitch and lure living men. Still another way is to interpret it as being constructed from light itself. Driven to the wood by the "fire" in his head, Aengus goes fishing in the twilight of dawn when "moths" fly and stars "flicker" out. This is the time of the day, in the twilight of dawn that Yeats always thought miracles are most likely to happen. Carrying the fish back to the fire in his hearth, he hears the silver trout transform into a "glimmering" girl who fades into "the brightening air". Grown old he still dreams of finding her, in imagery which resembles light and apple blossoms, but now the blossoms have matured into the enormous shining fruit which light all things.

The poem has rich sensuous imagery: hazelwand, "white moths", "moth-like stars flickering out", "silver trout", and "glimmering girl with apple blossoms in her hair". The climax of the poem's sensuousness is reached in the last two lines, describing the "silver apples of the moon", and "golden apples of the sun". The strength of the poem is formed from its nouns and deliberate repetitions and strong verbs: "peeled", "hooked", "dropped dream of successful love". This is what gives the poem its unique quality.

Adam's Curse

Yeats' long unrequited love, Maud Gonne, was the subject of many of his poems. "Adam's Curse" too is indirectly about her. The idea was sparked off talking to her sister Kathleen, at a time when Maud Gonne looked particularly dishevelled, and Kathleen, in comparison, looked immaculate. She had remarked that looking beautiful was hard work. This poem thus reminds us of God's curse to Adam that anything worth achieving had to be acquired through hard labour. The poem looks at three parallel examples – the attainment of beauty, writing a spontaneous poem, and winning over a lover.

The poem is written in heroic couplets, rhyming couplets in iambic pentameter. Some of the rhymes are full, and some are partial (for example, clergymen / thereupon). The poem is written in a conversational style, the rhythm suggesting the informal, easy atmosphere. Its stylistic simplicity and lack of heavily symbolic allusions adds to the appeal of the poem, making it one of Yeats' best-loved poems, and echoing the theme of the poem: a poetic line should seem "but a moment's thought".

The poem opens conversationally, with Yeats sitting with "that beautiful mild woman", Maud Gonne's sister and her. They talked of poetry, and Yeats commented that however difficult writing may be, "take us hours", it ought to appear spontaneous. He illustrates two images, both of people doing the hardest physical labour, scrubbing a pavement, and breaking stones, and to oppose it is an image of a poet writing. He says that "to articulate sweet sounds together" is more difficult than this work. However, it is a thankless task, as the poet has to strive to appear that the poem is natural and effortless. "The noisy set" – bankers, clergymen, and school-masters think that poets are "idlers", feeling that they are the real martyrs of the world.

On hearing this Kathleen replies that to be a woman is to know, that even though one may feel that beauty is a gift, and may compliment her voice as "sweet and low", she knows that they "must labour to be beautiful". The poet here replied that ever since "Adam's fall", or the day when God gave him the curse, there is nothing "fine", "but needs much labouring". Even lovers have had to quote learned lines and declarations of love, "precedents out of beautiful old books". However, it is generally perceived as an idle occupation, and lovers are berated for being wasteful and dreamy, despite their elaborate coaching in the art of love.

Here the friends become silent and watch the "last embers of daylight die", as the beautiful sunset lights up the sky into a "trembling blue-green". Amidst this beautiful imagery, the symbol of love, the moon, "worn as if it had been a shell", grows weary and shines in the sky. Just as the "embers of daylight" symbolise the sunset, and the "time's waters" symbolise the tide, the weary moon represents Yeats' love – still beautiful but deluded and misty. His heart is as weary and worn as the moon.

Yeats here voices a thought meant for Maud Gonne's ears only, that she is beautiful, and that he had "[striven] to love [her] in the old high way of love". His tone speaks of disappointment and regret, probably as he felt that to win the heart of someone like her, he needed to make greater sacrifice and effort. He feels that he had not tried hard enough, and thus he had not been able to win her. Though the scene was happy, he was as "weary-hearted" as the "hollow moon", echoing his emptiness and disappointment.

The surprise ending of the poem is just how good conversation should be, and provides a twist to the ending. The mood of the poem is softened, and the rising moon is a metaphor for the effects of time on the wounded heart, a weariness compounded by the labour of living.

Wild Swans At Coole

W. B. Yeats, unlike many great poets of his time who burned out in their youth, increased his poetic intensity with age, and wrote most of his best poems after the age of fifty. This poem deals with themes of old age, linked to poetic inspiration and intensity. Yeats fears that as he grows older, he will lose his intensity of writing, slowly growing more desolate.

The poem "Wild Swans at Coole" is the title poem of a volume of poems published in 1919 of the same name. These poems dealt with a progression of themes – among them his dear friend Lady Gregory's son Robert, old age, and finally an elegy on Robert. Major Robert Gregory died in the war, and his death made an impact on Yeats, prompting him to ponder deeply on issues of old age and death, mortality and immortality, and the eternal cycle of life and death, which lead to the writing of this volume of poetry.

The poem is written in iambic meter, in five stanzas of six lines each. The rhyme scheme is *ABCBDD*. The solemn serenity of the poem comes from its beautiful nature imagery, the plaintive tone of the poet, and the carefully constructed stanzas, giving the poet an opportunity to pronounce short, heartfelt statements before a long silence.

The poem is describing a scene at Lady Gregory's estate, on one of Yeats' several visits there. The scene is set in autumn, where the trees reflect the beauty of autumn. The lake reflects "a still sky", and perching among the stones, Yeats counts "nine-and-fifty swans". The swans are a significant point in the poem, as they mate for life. The odd number reveals that one swan is without a mate, symbolising Yeats' fate. His lifelong love Maud Gonne continues to reject him, causing him deep pain. He too, like the swan, is without a mate.

The poem reflects the passage of time: nineteen years since he first counted the swans. Much has changed in these nineteen years – the First World War, the Easter Rising of 1916, the death of Maud Gonne's husband and her final rejection, his hasty marriage, and the death of Robert. The world is a completely different place, and along with it, Yeats has aged. In the midst of his count, the swans "mount" in the sky, "wheeling in great broken rings", perhaps anticipating his theory of the gyres. Earlier he was more carefree, and "trod with a lighter tread", reflected by the bell's ring. Now it tolls, as he carries a heavy heart.

The swans are equally "companionable" in either water or the air, symbolising their simultaneous existence on earth and in eternity. "Unwearied still", they seem to be immortal. Even though they may age or die, like Yeats or Robert, but they reflect a pattern, one which is timeless and immortal. "Their hearts have grown old", mirroring their timelessness; also reflecting Yeats' concern for his own mortality. He is fearful that his time is running out and that slowly so is his poetic creativity.

The "mysterious, beautiful" swans linger still, leading the poet to his final question, one along with many others he attempts to answer in his poems: where will the swans be, or what will they do "when I awake some day / To find they have flown away?" This question again reveals his fears and suggests more mysteries; the pattern of man survives, and some day he will find himself dead (awake someday). Or maybe he will live on through his poetry, immortal.

Yeats' pain of unfulfilled love led him to question many aspects of life, and the events of the preceding years brought thoughts of old age and death, leading to this poem. Not quite answering his questions, the poem throws up further questions.

Broken Dreams

"Broken Dreams" was written when both Yeats and his long unrequited love, Maud Gonne, were middle aged. Though she never reciprocated his love, she was his muse, and inspired him to write poetry, beautiful poems full of imagery and feeling. Though he is now old, and it has been many years, he still feels some passion for her. This passion is however mingled with feelings of disillusionment.

In this poem Yeats is speaking to Maud Gonne, telling her that there is grey in her hair, and she has grown middle aged – her youth has faded away. Men "no longer catch their breath" when she is passing by, and her beauty does not break hearts the way it used to. However, maybe some old man prays for her and blesses her, as it was her prayers that saved him "upon the bed of death". For her sake the poet's heart has been broken, and he in turn has broken the hearts of many girls. From the moment of girlhood, she was beautiful, but it brought with it a burden. Her effect, "portion of peace", was so great that she lit up a room as she walked in.

The poet is saying that her beauty has only left "vague memories" with him, as his love was never brought to fruition. A young man would ask an older man to tell the story of the lady, whom the poet "stubborn with his passion" sang of, tell the story of her beauty and his obsessive love.

Yeats then says that after death "all shall be renewed", they would meet again. He will see her walking, "in the first loveliness of womanhood", and with his former "fervour", he will love her again, "muttering like a fool".

The poet praises her exquisite beauty, however points out her "flaw". She had "small hands" that were not beautiful – metaphorically hands that were not generous, that did not reach out to him. He is fearful that she would "paddle to the wrist" in "that mysterious, always brimming lake" of love. She should paddle to the wrist, as above the wrist she is perfect. He is displaying a little bitterness here, along with some disillusionment. He knows that she will marry, he just hopes that there will be a little part of her, her hands that he has kissed, that she will leave unchanged, "for old sake's sake".

Yeats' disillusionment and unhappiness comes through in this poem, as "broken dreams", so does his positivity and eternal hope -- that they would meet again, even if after death. He would always love her, and he has faith that one day she would return his love.

The Second Coming

Yeats spent years developing a mystical theory of the universe, which he later explained in his book, "A Vision". According to him, a civilisation begins with a moment of inspiration, a revelation. It starts like a thread unwinding from a cone, with the apex being strong; but as it unwinds, "its energies dissipate", and it "widens" and tapers off. This process lasts approximately two thousand years. An opposing force, which has been gaining strength, takes over and begins a new civilisation. This is represented schematically by two cones, intersecting at the points, and is called a "gyre". The word produces a sense of a circling, "turning" motion, while "widening" suggests both increasing the scope of the movement and its uncontrollability. In this poem, Yeats draws upon his theory to describe the changing over from one civilisation to the next.

Yeats has used a rough iambic pentameter in "The Second Coming", so loose that it can be considered free verse. The poem's rough nature echoes the roughness of the civilisation being born. It gives an appearance of emotions gushing out. The first two couplets rhyme, the rest are considered half-rhymes, like "man" and "sun". The fifth line of the poem enjambs into the sixth, creating a feeling of a flowing "blood-rimmed tide", enhancing Yeats' feeling of disillusionment and panic.

Due to the stunning and violent imagery, "The Second Coming" is one of his most famous and most anthologised poems, although it is a difficult poem for most readers to grasp. The first stanza describes the present state of the world, while the second predicts the coming of a second civilisation, horrific as a nightmare, which is inhabited by creatures like the slouching "beast".

The opening lines of the poem show the disintegration of the Christian civilisation, and compare it to a falcon that has lost contact with its falconer (God). The world is falling apart, and there is no one stabilising force. "Anarchy is loosed upon the world". Amidst this confusion, the tide of sexual and social violence is flooding everything, including the ceremony of innocence. The poet implies here that not even baptism is sufficient to rinse the sins of the people, and in fact is just as sullied. Fanatical men have seized power, while better men, full of doubt, are being ruled by them. The normal order of the world has been wholly reverted.

The poet feels that "surely some revelation is at hand"; the revelation that will give rise to the second civilisation, "the second coming". The reference to "Spiritus Mundi" is another concept of Yeats, stating that there exists a powerful storehouse of images that have a meaning of their own, and yet helps determine and predict events in the future. A poet or philosopher only has to respond and accept the signs. The image he sees is of a horrible, "rough beast", with the head of a man and the body of a lion, devoid of all emotions, with a "pitiless" gaze. This creature represents mindless and merciless violence; the creature moving "its slow thighs" conveys the clumsy, powerful stirring of the creature into life. Around this beast "reel" vultures, symbols of death and destruction, foretelling the future of the effect of the beast upon the world. For "twenty centuries" this beast has been gestating, only to emerge now, "its hour come round at last". Ironically, it moves towards Bethlehem, the birthplace of Jesus, going to be born as the "anti-Christ", starting its new civilisation from the same place as the earlier one.

This poem was written by Yeats describing the current historical context, appearing against the monstrosities of the First World War, and its effect on the entire world. He felt that the next age would take as its ideals not the concepts of science, democracy and freedom, but mysticism, primal power and captivity. The future of the rising sphinx is his vision of the character of the new world, a character so horrific. The poem is about the opposing forces between the modern world and the Christian era. It may not thematically represent Yeats' best work, but its aesthetic experience and passionate language assures its place among Yeats' finest poems.

A Prayer For My Daughter

Yeats wrote "A Prayer for My Daughter" shortly after "The Second Coming", and in the volume of poems they are published in, they feature one after the other. Yeats intended them to be compared and contrasted. As in "The Second Coming", he fears a "beast" being born, and ruling the world. He fears the future for innocents like his daughter. How will they be able to escape the wrath of the coming times? He feels that it will only be possible through "custom and ceremony".

The poem opens with an image of a child sleeping innocently through a howling storm. The storm that originated from the Atlantic is "levelling the countryside". Amidst this, the poet has been walking and praying for an hour, due to the "great gloom" in his mind, his concern for the happiness of his daughter. The coming of the storm portents the dark times ahead and the crisis of morality faced by the human race. The poet senses this, and prays to protect his daughter from the inevitable.

Yeats hears "the sea-wind scream", and the stream beneath his tower is "flooded". The violence of nature seems symbolic of a larger violence, "the murderous innocence of the sea", the symbol of which in "The Second Coming" had been the "blood-dimmed tide". He is "imagining in excited reverie" how his child will be nurtured in such an atmosphere. Yeats balances the real storm against the symbolic storm in the future which will threaten the existence of man.

Yeats prays that his daughter be "granted beauty", yet not be so beautiful as to make a "stranger's eye distraught". He feels that historically beautiful women feel that their external appearance is sufficient, and overtook the inner beauty of "natural kindness" and "heart-revealing intimacy". He cites the example of Helen of Troy, who fell in love with a "fool", and caused a war, and Aphrodite, who "could have her way", yet chose Hephestay, physically imperfect. To him beauty and idiocy go hand in hand. He is making an oblique reference to his lifelong love Maud Gonne, who made wrong choices, causing unhappiness for herself, and never really "[found] a friend".

Yeats would rather have his daughter take after her mother, and learn that "hearts are not had as a gift, but hearts are earned". He hopes that she will escape the sort of "intellectual hatred" that turned Maud Gonne into a jailed propagandist, her once lovely voice turned into "an old bellows full of angry wind". He focuses the poem on two images: that of the "Horn of Plenty" which he associates with courtesy, aristocracy and ceremony, and the laurel tree, which represents reality and happiness, "rooted in one dear perpetual place". He hopes she blossoms and flourishes like the tree, her thoughts cheerful like the songs of the linnet; not creating friction but contributing to love and generosity in the world. She should not quarrel but in jest, and be competitive only for the sake of fun.

Yeats next talks of Maud Gonne and her mind "choked with hate" for the British. He believes that such a person will never find happiness. Though born with everything desirable, due to "her opinionated mind" she turned her life into a bitter one, full of suffering and hostility. The poet believes that if a person is able to purge all hatred from their mind, their soul will recover its original innocence, and despite all hostilities they face externally, "though every face should scowl", they will be happy.

Yeats greatly believes in tradition, and hopes that his daughter marries into a traditional home, rooted in values and "customs". Custom and ceremony here are opposed to hatred and arrogance, and give birth to innocence and beauty. Yeats believes in formal courtesy and etiquette, and does not subscribe to the crude attitudes subscribed to by the socialists.

In the troubled times following the first World War, Yeats is deeply concerned about the well-being and happiness of his daughter, and thus writes this poem. He has wasted years on a futile love for Maud Gonne and is now disillusioned. He sincerely hopes that his daughter will not be like Maud Gonne, who according to Yeats, wasted her life making wrong choices and filling her heart with hatred instead of love. He wishes that his daughter lives a far more fulfilled and happy life.

In this poem, Yeats addresses his fears and hopes for his newly born daughter, as well as laments his lost love. He hopes his daughter will be loving and kind, unlike the woman who broke his heart. This woman had so much hatred in her heart; she had no space left for love. He writes this poem as a wish, a prayer, one that he releases into the wind, as he does his lost love.

STUDY GUIDE

MULTIPLE CHOICE QUESTIONS

W.H. Auden

1. When was W. H. Auden born?
 a) 21 February 1907
 b) 7 May 1905
 c) 20 August 1906
 d) 22 December 1904

2. Where was Auden born?
a) London
b) Manchester
c) York
d) Birmingham

3. Which university did Auden attend?
 a) Edinburgh
b) Cambridge
c) London
d) Oxford

4. Which poem won Auden the Pulitzer Prize in 1948?

a) The Double Man
b) The Age of Anxiety

c) Night Mail
d) Journey to a War

5. Which country did Auden become a citizen of in 1946?
a) France
b) Austria
c) England
d) America

6. Where did W. H. Auden die?
a) London
b) Birmingham
c) New York
d) Vienna

7. Auden's poem "Lullaby", is about
a) Emotional love
b) Physical love
c) Metaphysical and spiritual love
d) Platonic love

8. The title of the poem "Musee des Beaux Arts" refers to the:
a) Louvre Museum in Paris
b) Museum of Fine Arts in Brussels

c) Museum of Modern Art in New York
d) The Van Gogh Museum in Amsterdam

9. The poem "Epitaph on a Tyrant" is influenced by the tyranny of:
a) Benito Mussolini

b) Joseph Stalin
c) Adolf Hitler
d) Genghis Khan

10. The poem "The Unknown Citizen" is about:
a) The plight of the Jews
b) The dehumanization of society
c) The tyranny of those in power
d) The futility of ambition

Ted Hughes

1. Where was Ted Hughes born?
a) Warwickshire
b) Yorkshire
c) Wales
d) Berkshire

2. Which university did Hughes attend?
a) Oxford University
b) Cambridge University
c) Edinburgh University

d) He didn't attend university at all

3. The name of Hughes' first wife was:
a) Assia Wevill
b) Carol Orchard
c) Sylvia Plath
d) Elizabeth Browning

4. Hughes received this award:
a) The Order of Merit
b) The Whitbread Prize for Poetry
c) The Guggenheim Fellowship
d) All of the above

5. Ted Hughes died in the year:
a) 2001
b) 1980
c) 1998
d) 2010

6. In the poems of Ted Hughes, animals are portrayed as:
a) pets
b) wild animals
c) metaphors for human beings
d) vulnerable to human cruelty

7. In the poem "The Full Moon and Little Frieda", the poet states that:
a) Children are at a sharp contrast to nature
b) Children are drawn to nature and a part of it
c) Children are more valuable than the natural world
d) The natural world is superior to human beings.

8. The poem "The Thought-Fox" is a poem about:
a) Fox-hunting
b) The beauty of nature
c) The process of inspiration
d) The superiority of man

9. The poem "Wind" describes:
a) The strength of nature's fury
b) The vulnerability of man when faced with nature
c) The metaphor of a relationship between a man and a woman
d) All of the above.

10. Hughes' work is well-known for its:
a) Lyrical imagery
b) Use of the sonnet form
c) Alliterative devices
d) Portrayal of the beauty and violence of nature

John Keats

1. When was John Keats born?
a) 22 June 1755
b) 16 August 1785
c) 31 October 1795
d) 31 December 1801

2. Where was Keats born?
a) Paris
b) Berlin
c) Moscow
d) London

3. Which profession did Keats apprentice in but never practiced?
a) Law
b) Architecture
c) Accountancy
d) Medicine

4. The number of significant odes Keats' wrote:
a) Four
b) Eight
c) Twelve
d) Six

5. What caused John Keats' death?
a) Malaria
b) Tuberculosis
c) Pneumonia
d) Cholera

6. In "On First Looking into Chapman's Homer", the poet claims he never really experienced Homer's work until...
a) he heard Chapman's translation.
b) he realised what he was missing out.
c) he watched an opera version of the story in London.
d) he translated it from the original Greek.

7. What form is the poem "On First Looking into Chapman's Homer" in?
a) Shakespearean sonnet
b) Petrarchan sonnet
c) Ballad
d) Villanelle

8. In "On First Looking into Chapman's Homer", the "realms of gold" are a metaphor for...
a) new planets
b) books of poetry
c) riches and treasure
d) heaven

9. The poem "The Last Sonnet", describes Keats' feelings of:

a) Falling in love

b) Realising his feelings were unrequited

c) His awareness of his mortality

d) His fear that he had written too many poems

10. The mood of the poem "To Autumn" is predominantly...

a) of anguish and uncertainty

b) calm and serene

c) full of strong emotions

d) full of longing

Philip Larkin

1. Philip Larkin was born in:

a) Warwickshire

b) Berkshire

c) Yorkshire

d) Hampshire

2. Larkin studied the following subject at university:

a) History

b) Political Science

c) English

d) Philosophy

3. Larkin's first published book of poems was called:
a) The North Ship
b) The Whitsun Weddings
c) A Girl in Winter
d) High Windows

4. Philip Larkin received this honour:
a) Title of Poet Laureate
b) Order of the British Empire (CBE)
c) Order of Merit
d) The Nobel Prize for Literature

5. Larkin also worked as a:
a) English teacher
b) Librarian
c) Accountant
d) Architect

6. According to the narrator of the poem "Church Going", what phase will come between the decline of religious faith and the total disappearance of churches?
a) Anarchy
b) Superstition
c) Prayer
d) Hatred

7. What does the narrator in "Church Going" mean when he asks, "what remains when disbelief has gone"?
a) Sooner or later, religious faith will conquer the doubters of the world
b) He actually wants to know what will happen when belief is gone
c) Superstition will take over the world
d) Once belief has disappeared, sceptics will no longer have anything to disbelieve.

8. The poem "Wild Oats" is about:
a) Agriculture and farming
b) Friendship and choosing the right friends
c) Choices between what we want and what we think we should have
d) Who we should love and who we actually love

9. The poem "The Building" is about:
a) Architecture
b) The mundane details of everyday life
c) The question of life and death
d) The best way to spend time waiting for others

10. The poem "Dockery and Son" discusses...
a) the poet's reminisces of the good times he had in school
b) the poet's desire to return to the safety of his childhood
c) the poet's reflections on his life choices and whether he made the correct ones

d) the poet's rivalry with Dockery in school

W.B. Yeats

1. Where was Yeats born?
a) London
b) Dublin
c) Sligo
d) Edinburgh

2. What language did Yeats originally write in?
a) Irish
b) Gaelic
c) English
d) French

3. Yeats' family came from what religious background?
a) Protestant
b) Catholic
c) Kabbalah
d) Atheist

4. Yeats was influenced by the writings of:
a) Shakespeare and William Blake
b) Dante Alighieri
c) Hinduism
d) All of the above

5. Which theatre did Yeats help found?
a) Peacock Theatre
b) Abbey Theatre
c) Gaelic Theatre
d) Dublin Theatre

6. Who was the love of Yeats' life?
a) Lady Gregory
b) Beckett's daughter
c) Sylvia Plath
d) Maud Gonne

7. Which modernist writer greatly influenced Yeats later in life?
a) Virginia Woolf
b) Samuel Beckett
c) Ezra Pound
d) James Joyce

8. Where was Yeats buried?
a) Paris
b) London
c) Sligo
d) Dublin

9. The poem "Adam's Curse" provides the central message that...
a) Life is essentially meaningless

b) Things come easy to some people

c) Anything worth achieving comes from hard work

d) The past holds important lessons for us.

10. Yeats developed a mystical theory of the universe, which he described in his book:

a) A Prophecy

b) Wild Swans at Coole

c) A Vision

d) The Second Coming

ANSWER KEY

W.H. Auden

1. 21 February 1907
2. York
3. Oxford
4. The Age of Anxiety
5. America
6. Vienna
7. Metaphysical and spiritual love
8. Museum of Fine Arts in Brussels
9. Adolf Hitler
10. The dehumanization of society

Ted Hughes

1. Yorkshire
2. Cambridge University
3. Sylvia Plath
4. All of the above.
5. 1998
6. Metaphors for human beings.
7. Children are drawn to nature and a part of it
8. The process of inspiration
9. All of the above.
10. Portrayal of the beauty and violence of nature

John Keats

1. 31 October 1795
2. London
3. Medicine
4. Six
5. Tuberculosis
6. He heard Chapman's translation.
7. Petrarchan sonnet
8. Books of poetry
9. His awareness of his mortality
10. Calm and serene

Philip Larkin

1. Warwickshire
2. English
3. The North Ship
4. Order of the British Empire (CBE)
5. Librarian
6. Superstition
7. Once belief has disappeared, sceptics will no longer have anything to disbelieve.
8. Choices between what we want and what we think we should have
9. The question of life and death
10. The poet's reflections on his life choices and whether he made the correct ones

W.B. Yeats

1. Dublin
2. English
3. Protestant
4. All of the above
5. Abbey Theatre
6. Maud Gonne
7. Ezra Pound
8. Sligo
9. Anything worth achieving comes from hard work
10. A Vision

SHORT QUESTIONS

W.H. Auden

1. Do you think that the poem "Musée Des Beaux Arts" is actually about the myth of Icarus? Or about Brueghel's painting? Is there a difference between the two?
2. What does the poem "Musée Des Beaux Arts" tell us about choices? Compare the indifference showed by nature and animals versus that shown by the humans in the poem.
3. How does the form (its meter, rhyme scheme, etc.) of the poem "Lullaby" affect its meaning?
4. Does the speaker in the poem "Lullaby" have a negative or realistic view of love?
5. The poem "The Unknown Citizen" was written in 1939, and some critics have found parallels with the rise of fascist, authoritarian governments in Europe. Is the "State" of the poem a fascist state, or is it merely a subtle parody of democratic and socialist governments?

Ted Hughes

1. What moral lesson does Hughes teach us in "Stag"?
2. In "The Thought-Fox", how does the fox illustrate the process of inspiration and creativity?
3. What aspect of human behaviour does the crow in "Crow Tyrannosaurus" illustrate?

4. Explain the relationship between humanity and nature in "Wind".

5. In what way does the poem "Wind" demonstrate conflict in human relationships?

John Keats

1. In the poem, "On First Looking Into Chapman's Homer", what is the difference between "realms," "goodly states," and "kingdoms" and the land in the second half of the poem?

2. In the above poem, what does the contrast between Cortez and his men tell us about Keats's view of his poetic calling?

3. In the poem "To Autumn", which parts of nature does Keats choose to represent in the poem?

4. Does the mood or tone of the speaker change at all throughout the poem "To Autumn"?

5. In the poem "La Belle Dame Sans Merci", what is the message that the poet gives us about love? Is he saying that it is manipulative and one-sided, or equally requited?

Philip Larkin

1. In the poem "Church Going", what is its overall take on religion? Does the speaker end up becoming a believer in the end?

2. What is the difference between spirituality and superstition in the poem "Church Going"? How are the two connected?

3. What are the questions about his own life that the poet asks himself in "Dockery and Son"? Do you think the answers make him regret his own choices?

4. In the poem "The Whitsun Weddings", in what way is the train journey a metaphor for marriage?

5. What does the poem "Reasons for Attendance" say about relationships?

W.B. Yeats

1. How does the style of "Adam's Curse" mirror its explicit statement about beauty? How does it connect the labour of living with weariness in life and in love?

2. What do you think of the concept of the gyre in "The Second Coming"? Do you think Yeats thought that the world was getting worse or better?

3. What is the relationship of "The Second Coming" to the Bible? What are the major differences in the two worldviews?

4. Do you think the poem "The Wild Swans at Coole" is about nature and the beauty of the swans, or do you think it is about something else?

5. What does Yeats most hope for, for his daughter, in the poem "A Prayer for My Daughter"? Who does he not want her to be like?

ACKNOWLEDGEMENTS

THIS BOOK WAS POSSIBLE because of the amazing English teachers I had in high school, who instilled in me the love of poetry and literature. I especially want to thank Cathy Ma'am and Payal Ma'am, who brought alive the world of nineteenth and twentieth century British poetry and literature.

This book was also the first book I ever wrote - when I was in my final year of high school. It wouldn't have been possible if not for the access to the British Council Library and its vast trove of books for budding writers. For this, and for introducing me to the world of books from before I could read, I want to thank my mom, who gave me the love of learning and the passion for books. She also accompanied me to the publisher's book fair, to gain contacts to get this book published. Although I was unable to get publishers interested, I did get a commission to write my second book, which was my first published book, released in 2005.

I also want to thank the various self-publishing initiatives that have enabled authors like me to publish books that we believe should be available to readers to read and enjoy. Along the way, I was also immensely helped by the writing of numerous bloggers and authors, and although I cannot list them all here, I am indebted to them for showing me the way.

ABOUT THE AUTHOR

Geetanjali grew up in India, spending her early years in Kolkata, and attending high school in New Delhi, where she first studied the poets featured in this book. She read law as an undergraduate at the University of Warwick, United Kingdom, and went on to get a Masters' in Public Administration from Cornell University, US, with a concentration in human rights and social justice.

Geetanjali's first book, "Seamus Heaney: Select Poems", is currently in its 6th edition, published by Rama Bros. India. Geetanjali currently lives in Singapore.

Contact the Author:
Email: geetanjalimukherjee.author@gmail.com
Twitter: @geetmuk
Facebook: www.facebook.com/geetumuk

Printed in Great Britain
by Amazon